Carol and MArk.
Thank you very muc[h]
support. I still la[...]
book your mom gave me - "Why
Christians Love Jews" Go AU!!
Denk
1/18/17

Grief Diaries

THROUGH THE EYES OF MEN

Surviving grief and loss
from the male perspective

LYNDA CHELDELIN FELL
with
DAVID ALLAN JONES
STEPHEN HOCHHAUS

FOREWORD BY GLEN LORD
CEO, The Grief Toolbox
Board President, The Compassionate Friends

A portion of proceeds from the sale of this book is donated to The Magic of Life, a nonprofit organization working to avoid drunk driving injuries and death. For more information, visit www.themagicoflife.org.

Grief Diaries
Through the Eyes of Men– 1st ed.
True stories of surviving loss from the male perspective
Lynda Cheldelin Fell/David Jones/Stephen Hochhaus
Grief Diaries www.GriefDiaries.com

Cover Design by AlyBlue Media, LLC
Interior Design by AlyBlue Media LLC
Published by AlyBlue Media, LLC

ISBN: 978-1-944328-48-1
Library of Congress Control Number: 2016916483
AlyBlue Media, LLC
Ferndale, WA 98248
www.AlyBlueMedia.com

PRINTED IN THE UNITED STATES OF AMERICA

TESTIMONIALS

"CRITICALLY IMPORTANT... I want to say to Lynda that what you are doing is so critically important." –DR. BERNICE A. KING, Daughter of Dr. Martin Luther King

"INSPIRATIONAL.... Grief Diaries is the result of heartfelt testimonials from a dedicated and loving group of people. By sharing their stories, the reader will find inspiration and a renewed sense of comfort as they move through their own journey." -CANDACE LIGHTNER, Founder of Mothers Against Drunk Driving

"DEEPLY INTIMATE... Grief Diaries is a deeply intimate, authentic collection of narratives that speak to the powerful, often ambiguous, and wide spectrum of emotions that arise from loss. I so appreciate the vulnerability and truth embedded in these stories, which honor and bear witness to the many forms of bereavement that arise in the aftermath of death." -DR. ERICA GOLDBLATT HYATT, Chair of Psychology, Bryn Athyn College

"BRAVE... The brave individuals who share their truth in this book do it for the benefit of all." CAROLYN COSTIN - Founder, Monte Nido Treatment Centers

"VITAL... Grief Diaries: Surviving Loss of a Pregnancy gives voice to the thousands of women who face this painful journey every day. Often alone in their time of need, these stories will play a vital role in surrounding each reader with warmth and comfort as they seek understanding and healing in the aftermath of their own loss." -JENNIFER CLARKE, obstetrical R.N., Perinatal Bereavement Committee at AMITA Health Adventist Medical Center

"HOPE AND HEALING... You are a pioneer in this field and you are breaking the trail for others to find hope and healing." -KRISTI SMITH, Bestselling Author & International Speaker

"A FORCE...The writers of this project, the Grief Diaries anthology series, are a force to be reckoned with. I'm betting we will be agents of great change." -MARY LEE ROBINSON, Author and Founder of Set an Extra Plate initiative

"MOVING... In Grief Diaries, the stories are not only moving but often provide a rich background for any mourner to find a gem of insight that can be used in coping with loss. Reread each story with pen in hand and you will find many that are just right for you." -DR. LOUIS LAGRAND, Author of Healing Grief, Finding Peace

"HEALING... Grief Diaries gives voice to a grief so private, most women bear it alone. These diaries can heal hearts and begin to build community and acceptance to speak the unspeakable. Share this book with your sisters, mothers, grandmothers and friends who have faced grief. Pour a cup of tea together and know that you are no longer alone." -DIANNA VAGIANOS ARMENTROUT, Poetry Therapist & Author of Walking the Labyrinth of My Heart: A Journey of Pregnancy, Grief and Infant Death

"INCREDIBLE...Thank you so much for doing this project, it's absolutely incredible!"-JULIE MJELVE, Founder, Grieving Together

"STUNNING... Grief Diaries treats the reader to a rare combination of candor and fragility through the eyes of the bereaved. Delving into the deepest recesses of the heartbroken, the reader easily identifies with the diverse collection of stories and richly colored threads of profound love that create a stunning read full of comfort and hope." -DR. GLORIA HORSLEY, President, Open to Hope Foundation

"WONDERFUL...Grief Diaries is a wonderful computation of stories written by the best of experts, the bereaved themselves. Thank you for building awareness about a topic so near and dear to my heart."
-DR. HEIDI HORSLEY, Adjunct Professor, School of Social Work, Columbia University, Author, Co-Founder of Open to Hope Organization

"GLOBAL...One of The Five Facets of Healing mantras is together we can heal a world of hurt. This anthology series is testimony to the power we have as global neighbors to do just that." -ANNAH ELIZABETH, Founder of The Five Facets of Healing

DEDICATION

In loving memory:
Gloria Bender Andreas
Matthew Eugene Baldwin
Kevin Kyle Boos
Morgan Taylor Carr
Dottie Jean Cloutier
Maureen Coy
Chris Dafoe
Brad Downs
Samantha Downs
Lauren Kristin Fennell
Cassidy Alexis Gardner
Barbara Gershe
James Allen Harms
Katherine Hochhaus
Tita M. Hurtado
Judith Ann Jones
Big John Kelly
Vincenzo Libio
Ashley J. Rieck

CONTENTS

BY GLEN LORD

FOREWORD

What does it mean for a man to grieve? We have many stereotypes in our society when it comes to men and their emotions, especially those involving grief. Historically, we have been told by family, friends and the media that "real men don't cry." We have watched male leads in movies ride off into the sunset hurting, yet stoic and alone. As children we were told to buck up and shake it off, instead of being taught how to grieve.

Men are not the same, and their grief will not be the same. However, there are many traits that are attributed to men, such as tending to talk less than women, or working out their emotions through actions. Those are stereotypes and do not apply to all men.

Our society has been increasingly showing a more realistic vision of what it is for a man to grieve. We are beginning to see men who hurt and cry, men who grieve and share. Men are being taught that it is okay to display strong emotions when grieving. "Through the Eyes of Men" is another tool that reassures us all that men can cry, and that it is not only okay but actually healthy.

In just about every decade of my life I have experienced intense grief. When I was a teenager, my grandmother died. In high school, it was the death of a dear friend. My grandfather died while I was attending college. My firstborn son, Noah, died when I was in my early thirties, and my mother died when I was in my forties. I became well experienced with grief, and yet none of these experiences were the same, and my grief for each was unique.

I really began to heal as I turned to other men in my pain, and as I grew in my grief I began to reach out to others. As the executive producer of the Walking Through Grief series, co-founder and president of The Grief Toolbox and president of The Compassionate Friends, I have walked with many on their grief journey. This has provided me with the opportunity to witness how men grieve, really grieve. A good friend of mine lost his only son, and set off across the country to build birdhouses in every state. Why? Because each birdhouse was a concrete expression of his or someone else's grief. Healing occurred with each nail and hammer blow. Another fellow griever lost one child to suicide and another to a drug overdose. He walks across the country to share the message of "Love Life." I have witnessed countless men who sat in the back of the room for months before having the courage to speak about their pain and to find a room full of hope. Others showed up unexpected at a memorial walk to unburden themselves of pain they held tightly for years.

I also bear witness to the multitudes of men who still embody the stereotype "men don't grieve" and have pushed their grief deep inside and allowing it to fester, leading them on a journey full of destruction and pain. It sometimes manifested in drug or alcohol addiction, broken relationships, violence to themselves or others, or a life with little peace or hope.

Sharing and reaching out to others in pain is the hope in grief. Through these stories of heartache and survival, all men are given the permission to grieve the way they need. They understand that their grief is not unique to them, that it has been shared by others. This will also offer hope to the women who want to help and understand the men they love.

Grief Diaries: Through the Eyes of Men uses the unique style of sharing multiple men's stories from that tragic moment when their lives were forever changed. Real men share their hearts, their intimacy, and their families. The grief journey is followed all the way to where they have figured out what it means to them and their lives, for their love to live on in them and through them.

This is what it means for a man to grieve: to give yourself permission to feel what you feel. To do what you need to do. To experience what you need to experience and to recognize and accept that as long as you're not hurting yourself or others, you are succeeding on this grief journey.

My hope for you is that by reading this book you will gain the strength and the hope to know that even though your grief is uniquely yours, you are not alone.

Hope and love,

GLEN LORD
Executive producer, Walking Through Grief
President, The Grief Toolbox
President, The Compassionate Friends
www.thegrieftoolbox.com
www.walkingthroughgrief.com

BY LYNDA CHELDELIN FELL

PREFACE

One night in 2007, I had one of *those* dreams, the vivid kind you can't shake. In the dream, I was the front passenger in a car and my daughter, Aly, was sitting behind the driver. Suddenly the car missed a curve in the road and sailed into a lake. The driver and I escaped the sinking car, but Aly did not. My beloved daughter was gone. The only evidence left behind was a book floating in the water where she disappeared.

Two years later, on August 5, 2009, that horrible nightmare became reality when Aly died as a back seat passenger in a car accident. Returning home from a swim meet, the car carrying Aly and two of her teammates was T-boned by a father coming home from work. My beautiful fifteen-year-old daughter took the brunt of the impact, and died instantly. She was the only fatality.

Just when I thought life couldn't get any worse, it did. My dear sweet hubby buried his head—and grief—in the sand. He escaped into eighty-hour work weeks, more wine, more food, and less talking. His blood pressure shot up, his cholesterol went off the chart, and the perfect storm arrived on June 4, 2012. Suddenly my husband began drooling, and suddenly couldn't speak. At age forty-six, he was having a major stroke.

My husband survived the stroke but couldn't speak, read, or write, and his right side was paralyzed. Still reeling from the loss of our daughter, I again found myself thrust into a fog of grief so thick, I couldn't see through the storm. Adrenaline and autopilot resumed their familiar place at the helm.

In the aftermath of losing Aly and my husband's stroke, I eventually discovered that helping others was a powerful way to heal my own heart. The *Grief Diaries* series was born and built on this belief. By writing books narrating our journeys through life's challenges and hardships, our written words become a portable support group for others. When we swap stories, we feel less alone. It is comforting to know someone else understands the shoes we walk in, and the challenges we face along the way.

Which brings us to this book, *Grief Diaries: Through the Eyes of Men*. Men and women are wired differently, and nowhere is this more apparent than in the face of loss. The style difference has been the source of misunderstandings and wounded feelings for generations. So what exactly goes through the mind of a grieving man? That is what *Through the Eyes of Men* is all about: shedding insight into the world of male bereavement. Long overdue, I wish this book had been around when we lost our daughter, so I might have had a better understanding of my dear sweet husband's state of mind. Would it have prevented his stroke? I'll never know. But I'm comforted knowing that this book is now available to help others better understand loss through the eyes of the men they love.

Wishing you healing and hope from the Grief Diaries village.

Warm regards,

Lynda Cheldelin Fell

Creator, Grief Diaries
www.LyndaFell.com

CHAPTER ONE

THE BEGINNING

Tears have a wisdom all their own. They come when a person has relaxed enough to let go to work through his sorrow. They are the natural bleeding of an emotional wound, carrying the poison out of the system. Here lies the road to recovery.
-F. ALEXANDER MAGOUN

Grief and sorrow is unique to each individual as his or her fingerprint. In order to fully appreciate one's perspective, it is helpful to understand the journey. In this chapter each writer shares that very moment when he lost his loved one to help you understand when life as he knew it ended, and a new one began.

*

CHUCK ANDREAS
Chuck's 60-year-old wife Gloria
died unexpectedly from heart disease in 2014

I will never forget the night before Gloria passed away. I worked second shift and would get home after 1 a.m. That night when I got home, Gloria was awake, which was unusual. She said she didn't feel well, and was going to bed. We went to kiss and she said "Don't kiss me on the lips, I might be coming down with the flu." So I kissed her on her forehead. We exchanged "I love you" and she went to bed. I sleep on the couch because I snore and need to keep the TV on. I woke up and looked at the clock and it said 11:20 a.m. That was strange, because Gloria usually woke around 9 a.m. to have coffee and watch TV. I called her name, and there was no response. I noticed the bedroom door was open. I called again, and as I walked through the door I saw that she had passed away. After screaming and fumbling with the phone trying to dial 911, I called and asked for help. To this day, entering the bedroom and seeing my wife passed is a vision that sticks in my head, and will until the day I die.

*

JEFF BALDWIN
Jeff's 20-year-old son Matthew died
in a drowning accident in 2011

Matthew had just turned twenty in June 2011 with ambitions of joining the military, and was working on losing twenty-five pounds in order to enlist. He was living with his grandparents at the time. He was coming to grips with his addiction to alcohol and smoking pot, and knew that he needed to clean up his act if he was going to be accepted by the military.

Matt had a strong desire to travel and see new places while serving in the military, and although he had quit school at seventeen, he wanted to go back and receive his high school diploma from the same high school that he had dropped out of, he didn't want just a GED from the technical college. So, through a program similar to the GED that the school had in place, Matt did indeed finish and received his high school diploma from Walter Williams High School, which he was proud of. To him, I think it was taking a wrong decision and making it right. Who says you can't go back and make it right?

On July 28, 2011, one of Matt's friends came knocking on his grandparents' door late that night, inviting him to a party his friend was having at his house. The friend was home alone for an entire week while his mother vacationed in White Lake, North Carolina, on her honeymoon, so Matt's friend had the house to himself. I was later told by police detectives that there were fourteen or more people at the party ranging from age thirteen to twenty. Most of the kids had brought prescription drugs from home, all of which they took from their parents' medicine cabinets. They called it a "pharm party," short for pharmaceutical party. All the drugs are removed from their bottles, poured into a bowl and then mixed up so that when the kids take a pill from the bowl they have no idea what kind of reaction or feeling they will have from the pill. Just imagine all those bottles poured into one bowl, mixed, and then passed around the circle of people in attendance. What a dangerous situation in the making. Somehow they managed to get alcohol from one of the friends who was over twenty-one, so they had all the alcohol they wanted in addition to marijuana and the drugs that some of the young adults ingested for themselves.

The next morning, my son Matthew was found floating just after 6 a.m. in an above-ground swimming pool. He was a perfect swimmer and had spent summers at his grandparents who had an in-ground swimming pool, and was taught how to swim from a very early age. Matt's death was listed as an accidental drowning. I knew I would have to wait until the toxicology report came back before I would know exactly what had led up to this deadly chain of events that claimed my son's life.

The detective assigned to the case was not forthcoming with news, so I found myself in the position of calling her and leaving messages on a regular basis in order to be taken seriously. Eventually I was told that each person who went to the party was rounded up and arrested for contributing to the delinquency of a minor. They were all released to their parents a few hours later. The autopsy showed that my son had taken a deadly combination of alprazolam (Xanax) and a large volume of alcohol which rendered him unconscious in the early hours of July 29, 2011. Essentially he passed out and slipped below the water surface. My world was forever changed that day, and I couldn't understand why this was happening. You see, in February of that year I had lost my mother. She was my best friend and we shared a special bond, and then five short months later, while I am still grieving the loss of my mom, I lose my baby boy! I had to put my grieving on hold for my mother and focus my attention on the loss of my son. Until this day I never grieved another moment for my mother because of my new loss.

A short twenty-one months later I endured another tragic loss when my sister, who was only fifty-four, died from an accidental overdose of methadone which was prescribed by her doctor. At this point I had lost everyone in my immediate family. I was the only one left aside from my daughter, who was now twenty. I have so much anxiety thinking about all the what-ifs, and I'm constantly thinking that something could happen to her as well. I just don't think I could bury another child again. The one constant I can say with a thousand percent certainty is that my faith in God is the only thing that has brought me this far in my journey.

I still have moments when I break into tears. Sometimes a song or a memory will trigger the sadness or pain. However I have tried to do a lot of positive things like forming my own grief support groups for mothers and fathers on Facebook called Mending Hearts Grief Support Group, for parents who have lost a child. It's a place for parents to go, and every member knows the pain of losing a child firsthand. It's a small group of about three hundred and forty members from around the world.

I also created and contribute to a Facebook page that offers information and helps teens and adolescents gain a much needed awareness of the dangers of alcohol and all the drugs out there today. It's called New Outlook Drug and Alcohol Awareness. My ambition is to some day go into middle and high schools and share my story and spread the awareness to all these young adults in the making. I plan to spend the rest of my journey helping others and hopefully saving some lives along the way. Bottom line, life is about helping others.

*

ROBERT BOOS
Robert's 21-year-old son Kevin
was killed by a drunk driver in 2015

I have been so lucky to have three amazing children. All unique, talented and of good character and gentle heart. Losing one of them is unthinkable, yet it happened.

I had just been home in south Florida for a weekend, and was on my way back to Arizona where I live and work. Kevin had gone to Tallahassee for Florida State's opening weekend football game so I didn't get to see him. As I landed, I received urgent text messages from my girlfriend, Michelle, and from my son Jeffrey: "Call right away, Kevin has been an accident." I saw the messages just before landing, and the next ten minutes were the longest ten minutes of my life.

I can't even remember who I called first or what I found out. I knew Kevin had been in a car accident, and that's all we knew. I called Kevin's mother who was in Tallahassee; she was on her way to Tallahassee Memorial Hospital to find out what was going on. I called the hospital and was transferred around multiple times. Nobody would tell me anything except that there were multiple traumas, but no names were given.

I got a frantic call from my friends Rob and Roxana who were on their way to Tallahassee because their son Vincenzo and his girlfriend, Morgan, were in the same accident. They didn't know anything either. I finally got home to Arizona and started waiting. Joy, Kevin's mom, finally got to the hospital but they wouldn't tell her anything; she was in the waiting room with a hundred Florida State University kids waiting to find out. Finally, the call came that altered my life forever; the call felt like a spear slid into my chest, and the pain will be there as long as I live.

It was Joy on the phone, calling from the hospital family room. No pretense, no build-up, no delay. "Kevin has passed away."

"What did you just say?"

"Kevin has passed away."

You might as well inscribe these four words on my tombstone now. Because they are already seared into my brain, words I will never forget. Words that I can hear now six months later, as if I just heard them six minutes ago.

Passed away. Died. Ceased to exist. Gone. Forever. Forever.

I'm not sure what I said after that. I'm not sure what I did.

They tell you that shock is real and your body goes into shock to protect you. I guess I believe this, because I don't remember the moments after hearing those words. I remember feeling chest pain. Sharp and deep chest pain. And nausea. And I couldn't breathe. I didn't tell Michelle or anyone, of course; I didn't want paramedics called or anything like that.

I just knew that no matter what, I had to get to Florida.

*

RODNEY CLOUTIER
Rodney's 21-year-old fiancéee Cattie was killed by a drunk
driver in 2013, and his premature daughter Dottie died in 2016

On August 20, 2013, my fiancée Cattie was out with friends as usual. The boys involved, I can't remember their names, but the driver was going down a 45 mph road with a hairpin curve that should have been taken at 10 mph. From the marks left on the road, the cops predicted the driver was doing 120 when he overcorrected on the curve, hit a driveway, and flew about a hundred feet. The car rolled several times. The driver and one of the passengers were buckled, but Cattie wasn't. What strikes me very odd is that Cattie herself wouldn't drive faster than the speed limit, nor would she ever get into a vehicle without putting on her seat belt.

The driver walked away. He faced manslaughter charges, a year in jail, and probation for ten years. There was a breathalyzer locking device installed in his car. As far as I'm concerned, he should still be in jail. As for the other kid, they dropped all charges because he went into a mental institution and still has mental issues. I feel bad for that kid. It wasn't his fault.

Then came the death of my premature daughter on April 10, 2016. Chelsea, my soon-to-be wife was pregnant with our first child. She was twenty-one weeks along and we already had a scare months earlier, so she was given orders for no lifting. I was unemployed at the time so helping her with my stepson wasn't a problem. At 3 p.m. that day I was in the garage working on stuff when her youngest asked me to help find her mom's phone, so I did. On my way back out Chelsea called me. "We need to go to the emergency room. I got sick and I'm discharging a bunch of blood."

"Okay. I'll get the kids ready," I said.

I packed the diaper bag, got the pickup started and waited for her to rinse off. The emergency room was thirty-two miles away, a thirty-minute drive. We made it in fifteen to twenty minutes, driving 75 and then 80 mph in two different speed zones. I dropped Chelsea off at the emergency room door, parked the pickup, and brought the kids in. As Chelsea came back from giving a urine sample she gushed fluid everywhere. She told the nurse who brought her a wheelchair, and up we went to the nursery. Chelsea's obstetrician was called and came in to get details. She then asked me to leave so she could do a special exam. I took the kids out and fifteen minutes later the doctor came out. She looked at me and said, "Chelse has requested you to get hold of her mom, and Sonny for the kids. I'm sorry, Rodney, you're going to lose her."

I was crushed, devastated, shocked and in total disbelief. She said, "I'll watch the kids. Go tend to Chelsea." Chelsea was so upset and I felt helpless because all I wanted to do was take her pain away and I couldn't. I called my mom and Sonny, who said they will be there as soon as possible, and asked them to bring us some new clothes and so forth. My little sister came to get the kids and took them home. Mom stuck around. Sonny had bowling that he couldn't miss. I'm on the team and he is my captain so I knew, and it was okay. Dottie was born at 8:45 p.m. that day. She survived for an hour and half on her own until she passed away on my chest. She was eleven inches long and weighed one pound.

I forced Chelsea to go to Dotti's funeral on May 5, 2016. Whether she hates me for it or not, we needed the closure. My side of the family showed up because they live nearby, but all of Chelsea's family are miles away. We had Dottie cremated and her ashes sit on our mantel. We also got dog tag lockets with a picture of her, Dobson, and the words "Lost but not forgotten"

To this day I still cry, I still miss them. It doesn't hurt to talk about it and if you're reading this, you're trying to find a way to cope. Everyone mourns differently. I was introduced to death at a very early age and the only thing I can say is keep pushing through the day; find something that keeps your mind from dwelling on it. Seek your friends for guidance and above all keep your head screwed on tight; it gets better as the days go.

*

M.G. COY
Myrton's 56-year-old wife Maureen
died of heart failure in 2012

My wife had been a type I diabetic since age ten. She went into the hospital for shoulder replacement surgery. They refused to allow her to take her medication, and she got ketoacidosis. She was in the hospital over Christmas, and when she came home she seemed okay. After we had our Christmas, I got up Sunday to make breakfast. When I tried to wake Maureen, she was not responsive. She died in her sleep. :(

*

BILL DOWNS
Bill's 21-year-old son Brad and 19-year-old daughter-in-law
Samantha were killed by a drunk driver in 2007

I remember that night like it was last night. My Saturday nights and Cruising the Coast classic cars weekend will never be the same. October 6, 2007, started out like any other day. I was working part-time as a laundromat attendant and was scheduled to work that night. Before I left for work, I told my son Brad and his wife of three months, Samantha, that I loved them and told them to be careful if they went out that night because of the extra traffic on the coast due

9

to the classic cars and crowds. I got in my car and headed to work. Chris was a young man whom the kids brought home with them when they moved home. My wife Julie and I grew to love Chris as a son in the time he also lived with us. When I got to work Chris was headed home from Jackson, Mississippi, after his girlfriend broke his heart. He called me to get directions on how to get home. When Chris got home, his frame of mind was not very good. Brad and Samantha decided to take Chris to the car races to get his mind off his broken heart, especially since Chris was willing to pay for it. The weather that night was partly cloudy and it had been misting off and on and the race was canceled, so the kids decided to go to the movies instead. They drove home in Chris' truck and changed into Brad's car. Brad wanted to take his car because he had bought this car himself and it was his dream car.

Chris called me as they were headed to the movies at 8:50 p.m. I told him I loved him, and to be careful on the roads. I told him the same thing I had told Brad and Samantha about there being more vehicles on the road with the Cruising the Coast club on the coast; I warned him that there would be partying and drinking while driving. He said "Love ya, Dad," and hung up. When I got off work that night, I headed home after calling Julie. When I got halfway home I came upon a roadblock where the officers were detouring all the traffic to another route.

I called Julie and told her I would be late due to a horrific multiple car crash. I told her it was very bad, I had never seen so many emergency vehicles and flashing lights. The lights lit up the whole night sky. This was a spot of many crashes due to a large curve and a hill in the same place. Julie said she would call the kids to warn them to stay out of the area when they headed home. When I reached the other side of the roadblock, Julie called and told me she could not get the kids on the phone. She told me to turn around and go back to the roadblock, that she would continue to call the kids. I called Julie's brother and told him to take her keys and not to let her leave until I knew what had happened at the crash. I then turned and headed back to the roadblock on this end to save time.

When I got to the roadblock the officer there told me to go home. I turned around to leave and Julie called me again and said she could not reach the kids. I told her I would not leave until I found something out. When I got to the original roadblock, the officers there threatened to arrest me if I did not leave. Julie called again and said she had been calling dispatch and the hospitals trying to find out something. Julie got in touch with the hospital and they said that two victims had been taken to the emergency room. So I headed to the emergency room. When I got there I was trying to find out who the victims were. The whole time I was there, Julie and her sisters were on the phone trying to find out who was in the crash. I had asked the night nurse if she knew who the victims were, and while she was checking, I got the phone call that no father ever wants to get. Julie called me and told me that Brad and Samantha were killed in that car crash. Her words still ring loud in my ears. "Bill, our baby is gone. They all three are gone. They were killed instantly." I fell to my knees, crying out like my world had just came to an end.

The coroner came in the lobby and began to console me. He took me into the back emergency room and asked if I could identify Chris' body. He said unofficially that the driver of the other vehicle was also killed; she was impaired and hit the kids head on, driving eighty miles per hour. When I walked into the room where they had Chris, I looked at him through teary eyes and recognized the young man I had grown to love as a son. To see him like this was almost more than I could bear. My life as I knew it was gone.

*

JAMES FENNELL
James' 21-year-old daughter Lauren
was killed by a drunk driver in 2008

This writing describes a journey. This is a journey taken by some of us who are lucky enough to discover love and who are predeceased by the one in our heart. When the person predeceasing you is a child, then the experience is unique in that one never expects to outlive our child. In the natural course of life, we might expect to lose a parent, a spouse or sibling. But never a child!

Lauren was on her way in life! She had just met her first true love, and shortly before had graduated from high school. Never an academic like her younger sister, Lauren even pushed up her classes so that she could finish her requirements six months early. After a short six months in college, Lauren decided that she was ready for the business world. After a couple of hourly jobs in the food-related industry, she had just begun her first management position for a national chain, running a food court and café.

She and Mike, who is a manager in the same company, often ventured off into the wee hours of the night after work, as it agreed with their working lives. At times I warned them of the dangers of being on the roads that late but decided that they were two adults who should ultimately make their own decisions. The events that followed would change the lives of so many who were left behind. The wrapping covered her entire face from the end of the nose and below. All that was visible were her closed eyes and forehead. The rhythmic pulse of the ventilator was a steady reminder that this life support system was all that kept her alive. The second brain wave test had come back and showed no activity. All that separated her technical passage from this world was for our family to give permission to discontinue the support.

As her mother, sister, and I watched helplessly, we began to realize that it was time to say goodbye. I gently kissed her forehead and told her I loved her. Even now, eight years after the incident, it makes me tremble, as these moments will forever leave an imprint on my soul.

A mere twenty-seven hours before, Lauren had said goodbye as she and her boyfriend Mike were rushing to catch the last showing of a Will Ferrell movie. Amanda, her sister, had helped Lauren tint her hair hours before; she picked a reddish tint to go with her beautiful auburn hair and big brown eyes. Lauren had met Mike only months before, and everyone who knew her was delighted to see her so content and so much in love. As they drove off they looked like the happiest couple in the world.

The film started at 11 p.m. As mentioned, Mike and Lauren often worked into the night, and they were used to getting a late start when they would go out together. After the movie they took a late-night ride, as they often did. It would be her last ride. The vehicle operated by the intoxicated driver never even slowed as it went through a red light and struck her side of the car. She never had a chance.

*

JEFF GARDNER
Jeff's 18-year-old daughter Cassidy
was killed by a drugged driver in 2013

My eighteen-year-old daughter Cassidy Gardner graduated from Trion High School in 2013. She started college that summer at Georgia Highlands with dreams of becoming a plastic surgeon. The week before Thanksgiving 2013, Cassidy got a small tattoo on her foot. It was a diamond with the words "Follow Your Dreams." We spent Thanksgiving at my grandmother's, eating with the family as we always had. After dinner I returned home with my small kids while my wife, Tabatha, and Cassidy went shopping. Cassidy would finish shopping with her friend throughout the evening. We spent the next few days just watching football and spending time together.

On Sunday, December 1, I took my youngest daughter to Atlanta to meet her mom. Cassidy wanted to go with me, so we drove her car. She wanted to listen to Christmas music as I drove us there and back home. When we arrived home, Cassidy got ready to go out with her boyfriend from a neighboring county to watch the movie "Frozen." As she walked out the door, I told her to be careful and said "I love you." She said, "I will be home tomorrow, and I love you."

The following day, Monday, I went to work. As I got off work I was looking on Facebook and saw a post by a radio station that said all four lanes of Highway 411 was closed due to a wreck. Highway 411 is about forty-five minutes from our home. I looked through the comments, and people were describing how terrible it was. Then I saw a comment that said a dark Volkswagen Beetle was one of the cars. My heart dropped to my feet.

I sent Cassidy a message and got no response. I tried to call numerous times but she didn't answer. The time was now 4:45 p.m. and the post said it happened at 2 p.m. The friend I was riding with said, "It wasn't her, buddy. You would have already gotten a call; it was nearly three hours ago." I found temporary comfort in trying to believe what he said. When I got home I asked my wife if she had heard from Cassidy, or about a wreck. She said no, and tried to contact Cassidy, but still no answer. I kept telling myself I would have already been contacted, and that Cassidy must just be busy.

We went to town to watch the Christmas parade and returned home about 8:15 p.m. After saying prayers with the kids and tucking them into bed, my wife and I went outside to sit on the porch. At 8:35 p.m. I sent Cassidy a text message, "I need to hear from you! There was a bad wreck today! Hello?!" A few minutes later headlights came toward our driveway. The car pulled in; it was state patrol. I heard a familiar voice getting out of the passenger side. It was our preacher, Andy. He saw my wife first and I heard him say, "Where is Jeff?" As I walked toward him I could hardly breathe or hold onto the wall of the house; I knew why he was there.

Andy said, "Son, I got some bad news. Cassidy was in a bad wreck today and a DUI driver took her, son."

I fell to the ground asking God, "Why? What did I do to deserve this? Why?" How was I going to live? How would I tell her siblings and my grandmothers that Cassidy was gone?

The driver had run a stop sign on his road at 65 mph while on his cell phone, trying to cross straight across four lanes to another road, hitting Cassidy's driver-side door in the last lane. She died instantly.

*

MICHAEL GERSHE
Mike was 8 weeks old when his 28-year-old mom
Barbara was killed by a drunk driver in 1970
Mike was 33 when his 33-year-old best friend
Big John was killed in a drunk driving crash in 2004

On the evening of September 19, 1970, my father was driving us home from visiting friends on Long Island, New York. My three-year-old brother was sleeping in the back seat, my mother was in the middle front seat, and I was in a little wooden carrier since I was only eight weeks old. We were less than a mile from home when a drunk driver plowed through the intersection as we proceeded through the green light and T-boned our car. The force of the impact was so great that it pushed us into a telephone pole that split the front of the car in half. My brother was miraculously uninjured; my father had to get some stitches and was bruised. I wasn't so lucky. Nearly all my bones were broken and my skull was fractured. I was airlifted to a different hospital for severe injuries. My mother underwent surgery for her injuries but died the next morning, on September 20, 1970.

Fast-forward to college. While attending Ashland University in Ohio, I met Big John Kelly, who lived across from me during my sophomore year and his freshman year. Along with four other guys, we all became brothers over the next fifteen years. There wasn't anything we wouldn't do for each other, and although we came from different walks of life, we were family.

On the evening of May 1, 2004, Big John was leaving a bar in Lakewood, Ohio, when another customer, who saw him get into his truck, called the police. The first police car missed Big John. As the second one was in the process of pulling him over, Big John lost control of his truck and hit a tree on someone's front lawn. He was driving while intoxicated, not wearing his seat belt, and when his head hit the steering wheel, he broke his neck. Shortly after getting to the hospital, Big John died. As a survivor of a drunk driving crash that killed my mother, I never would have imagined that one of my best friends would die as the result of being an impaired driver. The last time I spoke to Big John was a week before his death, during the NFL draft right after the Cleveland Browns selected Kellen Winslow Jr., a pick he hated.

On May 1, 2004, I had to make the toughest phone calls of my life to let others know Big John was dead.

*

CARL HARMS
Carl's mother Myrtle died from malpractice in 2005
Carl's 56-year-old father James was killed by a drunk driver in 2007

We had just started a new year, and my mother was in the final phase of her procedures to improve her mobility. We were completely unaware of an FDA warning and notification to physicians regarding the same procedure that Mom was having. The physician performing the procedure was aware of the warning but felt that the extremely low percentage affected was not worth the warning. Unfortunately, and tragically for my family, my mother fell into that low percentage. The FDA warning indicated that the dye used in the procedure could have adverse effects if mixed with certain medications which were prescribed to my mother, but the physician failed to advise her of this. At this time, we were unaware that thrombosis and sepsis were setting in.

As Mom was slipping away and slowly becoming unaware of her surroundings, Dad took her to the emergency room. She waited an additional eight hours in the waiting room before being seen, and then she was immediately admitted to the ICU. Eight days later we had to make the difficult decision to take her off life support. This was the beginning of my nightmare!

After my mother's death in 2005, Dad was just beginning to turn his life around. He was smiling again, joking, and being his silly old self. After returning from one of his many visits with my sister in Hammond, Louisiana, Dad asked my thoughts about his moving to Louisiana to live with her. He said that my sister asked if he ever thought of moving to Louisiana, and he replied, "I'm not saying yes, nor am I saying no. Let me talk to Carl to see what he thinks." Before I could answer his question, he said to me, "Nobody's feelings are going to be hurt if you say no, little boy. I won't move if you don't want me to!" I let it roam in my head for two days as I weighed everything.

I explored the selfish and unselfish reasons and finally told Dad, "Unselfishly looking at the situation, I think it would be good for you, and it surely would help Tammy while she's finishing school." He told me not to worry and promised he would visit every month. To ensure me of this, he decided to keep his general practitioner in Jacksonville, Florida, who happens to be my general practitioner still to this day.

On Saturday evening, April 21, 2007, Dad left Jacksonville for Louisiana; I had last spoken to him when he called me from an I-10 rest area near Milton, Florida. At 3:36 a.m. Sunday, my father, James Harms, was killed in a four-car collision involving two separate drunk drivers on I-10 West at mile marker 35 in Gulfport, Mississippi. A young lady returning from a Stomp Event at an area casino, where she recalled drinking four Grey Goose vodka cocktails with Red Bull chasers and possibly smoking marijuana prior to driving, started the crash. On I-10 West approaching Highway 49 just before the Three Rivers Road overpass, she clipped the first car, forcing it into the concrete barrier, into the path of my father, and forcing her into the grass just off the interstate. As she was yelling obscenities at bystanders and began to run from the scene on foot, the second drunk driver crashed into the rear of my father's car at approximately eighty miles per hour, without attempting to slow down. The force sheared the seat pin, forcing my father into the windshield and over the rear seat, while still wrapped in his seat belt, and out of his pants.

The initial drunk driver was quickly apprehended using her vehicle registration. She was found hiding under the covers of her boyfriend's bed. She denied driving the vehicle, claiming a friend had borrowed the car. The second drunk driver had to be extricated from his vehicle and transported to a local hospital. He was uncooperative and intoxicated, and law enforcement had to get a warrant for a blood draw, which yielded a 0.10 percent blood alcohol content hours after the crash. The first drunk driver, who caused the initial crash, had a 0.09 percent blood alcohol content hours later. She first ran through a muddy field to her mother's house, and then to her boyfriend's house, where she was found hiding.

On Sunday, April 22, at 4:24 p.m., while I was sitting in my recliner, the home phone rang. The caller ID read: Harrison County Coroner's Office. A gentleman identified himself as Gary Hargrove with the coroner's office and he had one question.

"Do you know James Harms?"

Reluctantly answering, knowing that the coroner calls for only one reason, I said, "Yes, that's my father."

He said, "I'm sorry to inform you that James was killed early this morning on Interstate 10."

It was mostly a blur from that point on. All I remember was shock, crying, yelling, crying. I remember calling his phone multiple times after receiving the call, because I didn't want to accept that this was true. I hoped that at worst Dad was carjacked and someone else was behind the wheel, not my father! Moments later I received word that the authorities had someone in custody for drunk driving and fleeing the scene. Anger quickly sank in, then eased off to crying repeatedly, and then back to anger! For the next three years I would not leave my house. I had lost my foundation and had sunk into a dark depression to the point where I just wanted to give up on life. I would drag myself out when needed and travel from Jacksonville to Gulfport for hearings and constantly ask for answers, only to be turned away and overlooked every time.

Of the two drunken drivers, one was charged for DUI manslaughter and fleeing the scene. She was sentenced to ten years but was released after serving only four years. The second drunken driver was never even cited or charged. A year following the fatal crash that claimed my father's life, the drunken driver was involved in yet another drunk crash; he fled the scene of that crash. This time he was apprehended, charged with a first offense for driving under the influence, and turned over to Immigration and Customs Enforcement. He was never mentioned or charged by the Gulfport district attorney for his involvement in the crash that claimed the life of my father.

Realizing that I needed help, I reached out to organizations and quickly realized that most of them were focused so much on fundraising that I couldn't get the help I desperately needed. I finally discovered a local grassroots homicide survivors organization that offered group support, grief camps and counseling. I discovered that my healing came from sharing my pain, so I became committed to educating myself in advocacy and started taking Florida state training courses to become certified to assist victims in my community. I dedicated my life to becoming a victim advocate, and I continue to help others as a victim advocate with the state attorney's office for the 4th Judicial Circuit.

I continue to share and educate through my community awareness program IMPACT! On April 25, 2012, I was awarded Jacksonville's 2012 Courageous Victim Award. On April 9, 2014, I received Jacksonville's 2014 Outstanding Victim Advocate Award from the Jacksonville Mayor's Victim Assistance Advisory Council.

The citation read, "The Outstanding Victim Advocate Award is presented to Carl Harms, a victim advocate with Compassionate Families, Inc. Motivated by his personal experience as a homicide survivor, Carl helps individuals and families who grieve for loved ones whose lives were taken by violence. He also works to ensure that fewer people become victims of crime by educating young people about the dangers of drinking and driving," were the words Jacksonville Mayor Alvin Brown spoke that day.

*

STEPHEN HOCHHAUS
Stephen's 51-year-old wife Kathy
died from adult soft tissue sarcoma in 2011

My wife, Kathy, and I were living a euphoric life. I was eleven years older than her, and as she had always been in very good health we never expected her to get a cancer that would take her so quickly. We lived in Arizona but as the years went by we started to spend our summers near Calgary, Alberta, to help with her aging parents who had begun having health issues. We built a condo near where her parents lived, and on our last trip up in 2010, Kathy felt a lump in her thigh that she thought might have been caused by the seat of the new vehicle we had purchased.

While we spent the summer up there, the lump began to show up when she sat down, so we decided to have it checked out on our return to Arizona that fall. We went to the doctor and after an MRI it was determined that Kathy had an adult soft tissue sarcoma and we needed to see a surgeon right away. We did, and were told it was very serious, but Kathy wanted a second opinion. The second doctor ordered a biopsy and we were told that the best chance for survival was to amputate the leg at the pelvic bone right away. This did not sit well with Kathy, and she decided to go to the Mayo

Clinic in our home town. They offered her the possibility to save all or part of her leg, and she chose that route. She started radiation and chemo in November but the tumor was growing in size and wrapped around her thigh bone, vascular and nerve bundle. We tried to be as proactive as possible to enhance her chances for survival. We saw a nutritionist and kept a positive attitude.

We discovered that this type of cancer was so rare that only eighteen cases had been treated that year, mostly at Mayo. There was so little information to determine what treatment worked best. After six weeks of treatment, we had a couple of weeks before surgery and decided to fly up to Canada to visit her parents, since they were physically unable to come down for Kathy's operation. Just before we went, a full body scan was done which showed no spreading of the cancer. We felt very optimistic at that time, but while we were up in our new condo Kathy developed a cough that got quite serious and required a trip to the emergency room. That was when the nightmare truly began.

It was determined that her lungs were filled with tumors. After days of hospital testing, they realized there was nothing they could do. I will never forget the young woman doctor who came to tell Kathy that any chance for effective treatment had passed long ago. Kathy just said, "It is what it is." The doctor actually started crying, saying something about how she had never seen anyone so brave. I simply remember thinking, how can this be happening? Still, we thought if we could just get back to Mayo in Phoenix, perhaps they could try something to save her life. I struggled for two days trying to get things worked out before an air ambulance could fly us back home. Sadly, when we got to the Mayo we were told that they could do nothing and she had but five days to live. I doubt I shall ever experience five days worse than that. She left me on the fifth day as I slept beside her in the hospice home next door to the hospital.

*

DAVID JONES
David's 54-year-old wife Judy
was killed by a drunk driver in 2008

Our youngest daughter, Lara, was trying to decide which college to attend. She had narrowed her choices down to two schools: Bowling Green State University, where her mother went, and Anderson University which is associated with our church. Lara was seventeen years old and was getting ready to start her senior year at Olentangy Liberty High School in Powell, Ohio. They wanted to make it a girl's day out to visit Anderson University in Anderson, Indiana. I kissed Judy goodbye, hugged her, and told her to be careful. She had donated blood the day before. I told her that if she became tired, she should let Lara drive. Judy and Lara looked a lot alike, and both were artistic, compassionate, smart, and fun to be with. They were very close and for the last three years was our only child still living at home.

It was a beautiful August day, blue skies, low humidity, and not too hot. Perfect for a college visit. I went to work as usual, but this time my son, Mike, dropped me off at work because his car was in the shop. Before I went into the office, I stood outside looking up at the brilliant blue sky and thanked God for giving me the best wife in the world, four wonderful children, a nice house, and a job that I enjoyed.

Lara and Judy had a lovely visit to Anderson. Lara had one of her good friends from Meadow Park Church there to go through the sessions with, and Judy talked to the college president about earning a Ph.D. in theology remotely if Lara decided to attend Anderson. Judy thought it might work out to drop off course work, see the professors, and visit Lara every week or two.

Mike picked me up at 6 p.m. in the afternoon, and we had traveled only a block when my cellphone rang. It was Lara. She said there had been an accident. I started to ask the usual questions and she said, "You don't understand. It was a bad accident." I asked if I could talk to her mother, and Lara said, "Mom can't talk." My heart started pounding and I was filled with fear. I found out where they were, that Lara had been driving, and that it was not her fault. Then the medics arrived and took her cellphone away.

I did not know what to do, but knew that I would not be able to get close to the accident because traffic would be backed up on the two-lane country road they were on, State Route 42, a road that was heavily traveled that time of day. I had Mike drive me home so we could let his brother into the house because he had forgotten his key. They were both home from college over the summer and were scheduled to return to campus in two weeks, Mike to the University of Montana and Geoff to Humboldt State in California.

I called the Highway Patrol, but they had no information. I left Geoff at home to answer the phone, and had Mike drive me south on Route 315 toward the hospitals. Five minutes later the medics called and told me to meet them at Children's Hospital.

We arrived just after Lara. We could see them wheeling her into the hospital and we followed. They took her to a room where they had almost twenty people; there was someone there ready to triage every situation. She did not seem too badly injured, at least physically. She had a long cut down her leg and really bad bruising on her upper body. I talked to her, gave her a kiss and signed papers for her to be treated.

Then I saw a group of four people who were waiting for me. We went into a small room next door and when I declined to sit down, one of them told me, "Mr. Jones, we are sorry to inform you that your wife was killed instantly in the car accident." I was devastated. I had them just leave me alone and cried on the couch. When I regained my composure, I went next door and brought Mike into the room. When I told him his mother was dead, he crumpled onto the couch. I sat next to him and put my arm around him, but could not think of anything to say. Eventually I thought he would be okay, and I went back to check on Lara.

They had finished stitching her up when two state troopers came into the room to see me. One had Judy's beige leather purse, which was covered in her blood. There was also a small baggie with her wedding ring, a cross necklace, a credit card, and some money. They gave them to me and told me about the accident. They said Lara had done everything she could to avoid the crash, but the other driver was coming right at her head-on. She went left of center to avoid the other vehicle, but it kept going all the way off the road, hit a guardrail and bounced off, causing the two passenger sides to collide at 55 mph each.

Everyone had seat belts on, airbags went off, but Judy had no chance to survive. They thought the other driver was under the influence but would need tests to confirm. They took a statement from Lara and said they had several witnesses who saw everything and reiterated that Lara did everything right.

After they left I noticed that Mike had not come out. When I checked, I found that they had him on one of the emergency beds getting oxygen. I called Geoff and had him come down to the hospital. When he arrived, I took him to the same room and told him his mother was dead. He took it better than Mike, and soon we got Mike released and we followed Lara around while they ran scans to check for internal injuries. Four hours later they found no internal injuries and left us alone together for the first time. Lara looked at me and asked how her mother was. I had to tell her that her mother did not make it. She said, "That's what I was afraid of and was why I was crying." She had had her license only for seven months and watched her mother die right next to her in the car.

Next week, on the funeral home site to leave messages, I saw an entry made by someone who was driving a car behind the drunk driver and watched the entire event. The writer said that shortly after the crash, the clouds parted and a brilliant ray of sunshine came down onto our vehicle, and they felt like they saw Judy's soul go up to heaven.

Even today, I cry whenever I think about that image.

*

JOHN PETE
John's 71-year-old grandmother Tita died
from diabetes and a series of strokes in 1989

My beloved grandmother's death was not completely unexpected. She was in gradually declining health over a period of years, largely due to diabetes. It was a long and difficult struggle, both for my grandmother and for our family, including myself. I had had a very close relationship with her my entire life.

Her declining health began with a mild stroke from which she largely recovered but two subsequent strokes later on left her increasingly physically incapacitated and with the inability to recognize her loved ones. My grandfather continued to care for her at home until her health required that she be placed in a long-term care facility that could offer 24-hour medical care. She remained there until her death in 1989.

*

ROBERT RIECK
Robert's 18-year-old daughter
Ashley died by suicide in 2016

Ashley was eighteen years old at the time of her death. She was a very smart, beautiful young woman and an overachiever. Ashley graduated from college with her Associate of Arts degree from Ridgewater College on May 15, 2015, before receiving her high school diploma on May 31. She was accepted into the Registered Nursing program starting in the spring. Ashley was employed at Rice Care Center as a certified nursing assistant, and as a server at a restaurant. She always thought of others before herself.

The day Ashley died, it was morning and we were all at home. Ashley was the second oldest of five girls; her older sister, Alexa, was twenty, Kendra was fifteen, Kristen was eleven, and Katelyn was ten. At the time, Ashley was looking to move in with a friend and not live at home. Two weeks prior, Ashley was in the process of moving out because I did not approve of her dating an older guy who lived an hour from home. Because of that, she was going to move out; we had not talked in the weeks prior to her death except for a few texts.

The night and morning before Ashley died, my wife had been texting back and forth with her; I was not aware of this at the time. She sent a text to my wife early that morning at about 6:30 a.m., but my wife didn't hear it until about 9 a.m. as we were all sleeping. When my wife finally listened to it, she screamed "I knew it!" and ran out of the house. I didn't know what was going on. Ashley had scheduled the text delivery time.

Ashley explained where her car was and said she couldn't go on anymore. We found her car parked near the lake access close to where we live. She left her phone as well as notes to all of us on the car dash. It still wasn't registering to me that this was real; I kept saying that she was around the area or someone picked her up. We spent an excruciating several hours looking for her body in the lake. All the neighbors were helping and then the sheriff came. My mind said she was still alive. It was so weird being by the shoreline waiting, watching and praying that she would not be found dead.

Several of us went back to the house to use the bathroom, which took less than ten minutes. That's when they found her body. Prior to finding Ashley, the sheriff had told me that unless he took his sunglasses off and looked at me straight in the eyes, that there was still hope. When I pulled up, he started walking toward me and I noticed he was taking off his sunglasses. That is when reality set in, and I knew they had found her body.

I just kept screaming "No, no!" It was the worst day of my life. I have a lot of guilt because Ashley was mad at me. If I had known the issues she was having the night and morning before, I might have been able to save her.

For several years prior, Ashley had been in counseling for depression and I had tried to help. Ashley never felt accepted by her peers or others around her, even though she was loved by so many who told her often. I have lived with the guilt every day since her death that I didn't get to tell her how much I loved her, how beautiful and talented and how proud of her I was. I let my anger about her dating an older guy and not following the rules get in the way. The what-ifs tear me apart every day.

With all the accomplishments Ashley made over the year prior to her death, I really thought she had put some of the things from her past behind her. But I was wrong and it'll haunt me until I die.

Most days I am just numb inside with the guilt from telling her that if she was not going to follow the rules, she would have to move out. It was meant to encourage her to see that the guy she was dating was using her, and to concentrate on her education and not on a guy who did not have a job. Instead, I made her feel unloved and unwanted by me, her father, and that just eats me up inside.

I love all my daughters so much, and as a father I wanted what was best for them, but sometimes I guess what I feel is best is not what makes them happy. It is hard for a father to let go as they get older, and being a father of five girls maybe made me more protective. Most days I just move forward with a smile, pretending that I have moved on, but inside I'm a mess. Some days I just cry, and most days I find it hard to do things. I have to force myself to do anything.

If it wasn't for my oldest daughter, Alexa, I would not have gone on. She has been my strength when I feel so alone; she keeps me living. I see so much of Ashley in her as well as my other daughters. I might not know what each day will bring, but what I do know is that I, her sisters, and all her friends are left with this empty feeling inside. Without her here, there is a void and nothing will ever fill its place.

I just hope it gets better, for me and for all those whose lives have been touched by Ashley, though I'm not optimistic this will ever happen for me.

*

Treasure your relationships,
not your possessions.

ANTHONY J. D'ANGELO

*

CHAPTER TWO

THE AFTERMATH

Long for me as I for you, forgetting what will be
inevitable, the long black aftermath of pain.
-Malcolm Lowry

Following profound loss, the first questions we often ask ourselves are: How am I going to survive this? How can I cope? There we stand in the aftermath, feeling vulnerable and often ravaged with fear. How do we survive?

*

CHUCK ANDREAS
Chuck's 60-year-old wife Gloria
died unexpectedly from heart disease in 2014

Surviving is probably the only thing I have been doing since it happened. Everyone who had lived at the house has been gone for a while, so I was actually happy that we have a dog, a cat, and a bird. Because of them I had to get off the couch and start to take responsibility again. Every morning when I take the dog out I look up at the sky and say, "Good morning, Glor." I very rarely get through a day without shedding a tear, but now at least sometimes I can smile and shed one because of a happy thought or memory.

I was told by a friend that the initial time would not be as hard. After a couple of months when people stopped calling and dropping by as often, that's when it would get really lonely. I thought to myself that my friend didn't know what he was talking about, but he was right. Your friends and acquaintances have to go on with their lives, and that's when my inner struggles really started.

My biggest adjustment is dealing with the loneliness, going to the store, cooking, making dinner, being in the house, all those things *we* used to do. Now it's what *I* have to do. Wanting to do things like going out to dinner, concerts, simple things that two people do without thinking, now I can't. All my friends are couples, and being the third person is not a comfortable situation for me, so I just don't do it. I have to avoid showing emotions, so it's easier for me to avoid people, or if I do go out I stay for only a short period of time and then I leave.

*

JEFF BALDWIN
Jeff's 20-year-old son Matthew died
in a drowning accident in 2011

I remember being in total shock and not being able to hold myself together without tears and emotions. I stayed busy the first three to four days, scanning photos of my son and preparing a video and photo montage that I worked on for two days. It was to be shown at Matt's chapel service just before we left for the cemetery, and our final goodbyes. I threw myself into this project because I wanted my son's life to be remembered, and to show all the happy occasions that we had captured in those photos while on vacations, and the love that he had and the love we shared as a family. It was so physically and emotionally hard and draining. I wanted to be consumed in whatever I was doing so I didn't have to think about the pain. I remember being so tired on a few occasions that when I did allow myself to sleep, I slept sometimes up to ten to twelve hours. It would take that long just to regain my strength, and then the cycle repeated itself.

*

ROBERT BOOS
Robert's 21-year-old son Kevin
was killed by a drunk driver in 2015

About once in every person's life, he or she will experience a date in history that will stay with him, and will define his life and the life of his generation.

December 7, 1941, was the defining date of my grandparents' generation.

November 22, 1963, was the defining date of my parents' generation.

September 11, 2001, was the defining date of my generation.

As deep and scarring as these dates are for most people, the date of September 6, 2015, will stand above all for as long as I draw breath. On this day, my wonderful, amazing, happy and healthy son Kevin was killed by a drunk driver in Tallahassee, Florida, along with his close friend since boyhood, Vincenzo, and Vincenzo's beautiful girlfriend, Morgan. Vincenzo was twenty-two years old. Kevin and Morgan were twenty-one.

This was Labor Day weekend, and it started out as normal and happy as any other. About a year and a half prior to this weekend I had been promoted within my company and helped them open a huge office in Tucson, Arizona. This took me far from my home in southern Florida, but it was a unique and once in a lifetime opportunity for my career. I had traveled back to Florida for the holiday weekend. I still had my townhouse, where my son Kevin lived with his older brother Jeffrey. Kevin went to school at Florida State University in Tallahassee, but had recently transferred to Florida Atlantic University for his senior year to be closer to his brother. Kevin had planned a long weekend in Tallahassee with his friends for FSU's opening weekend of football, so I was not planning to see him that weekend.

The weekend was hot and muggy. I was able to work a football game on Friday night (I am a high school football official) and got to spend time with my family and my other children. As I boarded the flight on Sunday afternoon, little did I know how my life would change by the time I landed back in Arizona.

About twenty minutes before landing I felt my phone buzzing in my pocket. A bunch of text messages had uploaded to my phone as it connected to wi-fi. Since it was supposed to be in airplane mode, I quietly checked my texts.

From my older son Jeffrey: "Dad, Kevin was in an accident. I don't know what is going on."

From my girlfriend, Michelle: "Bob, Kevin was in a bad accident. Please call right away."

So began the longest twenty minutes of my life. I had no way to connect until we landed at the airport. I started playing scenarios in my mind. If he had a broken bone or needed surgery, I would fly right back to Florida to be with him. If he faced a long recovery, I would move him to be with me in Arizona. Hopefully it was just a fender bender and I would call and hear his cheery voice say, "Hey, Dad, it's okay. It doesn't hurt." But I never got to have that conversation with him. Or have any other conversation with him. At least not one in which he could reply.

The drive from the airport to home was a blur. I made about ten phone calls trying to get some information. I found out that he was taken to a trauma center in Tallahassee and his mother, who lived in Tallahassee, was on her way there. I called the hospital and managed to get connected to the emergency room nurse station. After checking, a gentleman came back on the line and told me they had no information and that they had "no names" yet about the accident. This is when the very first inkling that something was *very* wrong started to creep into my mind. Having worked for hospitals for over twenty-five years, I knew something was going on. Despite privacy concerns, once I had identified myself and gone through a few questions I was sure they would let me talk to Kevin, or at least tell me that he was there. But they wouldn't say a word.

Simultaneous to all this I got a call from my friend Rob. He and I had been very close friends for over fifteen years. We all coached baseball and all our kids grew up together. I found out from Rob that he got the same call about the accident, that his son Vincenzo, known as Cenzo, was in the accident and so was Cenzo's girlfriend, Morgan. That was all Rob knew. He and his wife, Roxana, were driving from their home in Fort Lauderdale to Tallahassee at that very moment. This was an eight-hour drive. He had heard that my Kevin had been in the accident and wanted to know if I knew anything. I did not.

I called my daughter Shannon, who was twenty years old at the time and Kevin's "twin." They were born sixteen months apart and were exactly like twins. Her roommates were driving her from Gainesville, where she went to school, to Tallahassee. She was in a panic. I couldn't tell her anything, because I didn't know anything.

Suddenly the phone rang and displayed an 850 area code; the caller was unknown. I thought about the area code for a second and realized it was from Tallahassee. It was 9:11 p.m. Arizona time, 11:11 p.m. eastern time, and about two hours after the crash. It was Kevin's mother, my ex-wife Joy, calling from the hospital. Good, we would finally get to the bottom of this, I thought.

Joy, who is a very deeply religious and empathetic person, did not try to work her way up to this news, ease into it or anything like that.

"Kevin has passed away," she said.

"What did you just say?" came out of me, even though I knew *exactly* what I heard.

"Kevin passed away in the accident."

I'm not mad at her for how she told me, but I will never, ever forget those four words. They might as well be engraved on my headstone, because they now define my existence.

I've always heard about shock and how the body protects a human being at a time of physical or emotional trauma. I didn't know I would ever experience it quite so acutely. From the moment those four words hit my ear, my world shattered. And yet I was calm. I didn't scream, yell, or drop to the ground in agony, as far as you could tell. But inside me, all of that was happening. I was instantly nauseated, dizzy, and had chest pain. I couldn't move. My girlfriend, Michelle, came into the room and asked me if Kevin was okay. She must have seen the look on my face.

I said, "He's gone. My son is gone."

Think for a moment about this situation. I had just found out that my son was killed in an auto accident. I'm two thousand miles from there. My daughter Shannon is racing toward this horrible news, and doesn't yet know about her brother. My son Jeffrey is home in south Florida, and also doesn't know anything other than there had been a crash. In a haze of shock, I called Rob and Roxana to let them know about Kevin. I dialed Rob's number, and Roxana picks up. This was surprising, because in the ten times I had called over the past hour, Rob had answered.

But suddenly Roxana said, "Hello?"

As I began to speak, I heard this horrible anguished scream in the background. I immediately recognized the pain of a father, because I was feeling the very same thing although I hadn't yet released it. The very first thought I had was that someone must have told them about my son. Our families have always been very close, and Rob and Kevin had a very special friendship. Rob was Kevin's sponsor at his confirmation. I was touched that Rob was so upset about what happened to Kevin. But that wasn't quite it.

Just minutes before I got the call from the hospital, the police department called and told them that their son Cenzo was in the same crash, and hadn't survived either. Police departments or hospitals generally don't release information, let alone something this horrific, over the phone. But knowing Rob, he was likely very persistent until they finally told him. He and Roxana were still hours south of Tallahassee, in the middle of the night, and now hit with that news. To this day, I still don't know how they finished the drive and got to the hospital that night.

Jeffrey's aunt Kendra was racing over to his apartment, and Shannon was still trying to get to Tallahassee. She called me a few minutes after I found out the news, but I couldn't tell her. I had to lie to my little girl, knowing that in about an hour her world would be shattered.

"Dad, have you heard anything?"

"No, Shannon. I am waiting to hear. They won't tell us anything."

Of course, that wasn't true. I did know. I knew the worst. After talking to Shannon, I was waiting for Kendra to get to Jeffrey so that I could tell him what happened. When I saw his phone calling me and heard his aunt's voice in the background. I knew I just had to tell him.

"Jeffrey, it was a bad accident. Your mom just talked to the doctors. It's really bad news."

My ever-optimistic oldest son went right to a best-case scenario, "Does he have to have surgery?"

"No. No surgery. I'm sorry Jeffrey. He passed away."

Even over the phone I could feel Jeffrey's transition from concern to shock. He didn't scream or fight about it, he just asked me what had happened. Unfortunately, I didn't know.

Later, I told him and his sister that I was getting on a plane in a few hours and would be there the next day.

*

RODNEY CLOUTIER
Rodney's 21-year-old fiancéee Cattie was killed by a drunk
driver in 2013, and his premature daughter Dottie died in 2016

After Cattie's death, I just worked and ended up changing jobs. Since it was now just me and my daughters, I had to make them my priority. When my daughter Dottie died, I had the whole family to deal with: the three girls, my son, wife, my mother, Chelsea's father, and brothers. My means of coping was holding Chelsea, and crying together.

*

M.G. COY
Myrton's 56-year-old wife Maureen
died of heart failure in 2012

I did not cope. I had found my wife dead on a Sunday morning when I went to wake her for breakfast. Both my daughters helped, and I withdrew to my bed. I didn't eat for days. Both girls were a great comfort at that time.

*

BILL DOWNS
Bill's 21-year-old son Brad and 19-year-old daughter-in-law
Samantha were killed by a drunk driver in 2007

Losing my three kids, Brad, Samantha, and Chris, in a crash caused by an drunk and drugged driver was the most horrendous event to ever happen to me. The only way I survived the initial aftermath was with the support of my wife, and the fact that we were both in shock. I remember going through the motions of preparing for a funeral, making sure Brad and Samantha had clothes for the funeral that we thought they would have wanted to wear, what shoes they would wear, how Samantha's hair should be fixed, etc. Chris' birth mother took care of Chris, so we really did not have to deal with his preparation. But he was still my concern, because in my heart he was my son.

Walking around in a fog, I was able to face each day only with the support of my wife and family. There were times when Julie fell apart. Since she was my wife, I had to support and comfort her, leaving my feelings and emotions buried deep within me. Honestly, I was not coping well; I was just going through the motions. Being the man of the house, I didn't want to show my emotions or appear weak. I focused on comforting Julie and Cindy, our handicapped daughter. Not knowing just how much she understood was a fear I also had to face.

At work, my fellow employees avoided me like the plague while others smothered me with emotion. It was hard to tell which was worse, being ignored and avoided, or being smothered by compassion. Yet I still felt I could not show my emotions for fear of totally losing control, and thereby cause Julie and Cindy to fall completely emotionally apart. The expectations I set for myself were so high that there was no way I could reach them, and it was slowly destroying my stronghold, tearing down the walls I had built to protect myself.

*

JAMES FENNELL
James' 21-year-old daughter Lauren
was killed by a drunk driver in 2008

In the weeks and months that followed the accident, I often visited the accident site and speculate on all the things that had to happen in such a logical order for such as accident to occur. If just one thing had been different, this never would have happened. What if the drunk driver had left thirty seconds earlier, or later? What if Mike had decided to turn the car around a few seconds earlier? What if they had decided to stop for coffee, or gas, or to put air in the tire? What if they had decided to see another movie, or if they had another conversation that would have taken them down a different road?

Why did everything have to happen in the manner it did?

It was August 28, 2008, Lauren's twenty-second birthday. It was also the day we were leaving to take Amanda to her freshman orientation at Towson University in Maryland. That evening, I had a dream that I was sitting with Lauren in the living room, and had asked her if she would mind if we were not home on her birthday, and if she would be okay if we had her party the following weekend. It had always been customary to have an outdoor barbecue and pool party to commemorate her special day, and also to mark the end of summer. Amanda's birthday fell on May 27, and her party, in many respects, marked the beginning of summer. In the dream that was plain as day, Lauren smiled at me when asked the question, and said, "Of course not, Dad."

The months following the funeral — April, May, June, July, and August — were all somewhat similar. My wife, Marian, received almost daily visits from one or two of her five siblings. Being an only child, I had only my elderly mother, who was having many physical problems while convalescing in a nursing home. My first cousins, many of whom were close to me, all lived in the Midwest, a thousand miles away. Marian refused to discuss Lauren in any manner whatsoever with me, and seemed to shut me out more and more with each passing day. She even planned a candlelight ceremony and applied to have a street sign put into place to honor Lauren's memory without including me in any of the plans. What had I done? Was not losing a daughter enough without experiencing such detachment and aloofness from my own wife? It was sometime later when I realized that although people may be comforting and caring, strength had to come from within.

On September 10, nearly two weeks after Amanda's orientation, I returned to Maryland to bring her back home to attend her grandmother's funeral. My mom had passed away, two days before her ninetieth birthday.

Things that one always thought would be heartbreaking, such as going through the belongings of a parent once they departed, become even more so when faced with the additional challenge of taking on the task alone. As my parents aged, I knew that such an event would likely appear in my life one day but I was comforted by the notion that my wife and children would be by my side when it happened. Other than picking out a few pieces of furniture she wanted one afternoon, my wife Marian didn't offer to help me close up the home. Lauren was gone, so obviously she could not be there. Amanda was at school in another state, a hundred and fifty miles away, dealing with her own pain and sorrow as well as trying to piece her young life back together again. Normally children find the challenge of being alone at school for the first time to be enough without the added pressure of losing a sister along with the family she had always known.

I found myself able to spend no more than two hours at a time going through my mom's belongings at the house. My mind continually flashed back to memories of my girls at young ages playing in the yard or enjoying themselves with their grandparents. These beautiful memories of days gone by now seemed far removed from my life.

The year 2008 would close with Marian informing me that she wanted to end our twenty-eight-year marriage. She said it was nothing I had done; I was a "good man" and a "great father." It was about her, not me. I urged her to seek counseling, but she wanted to end everything.

So here I was on January 1, 2009, facing a "new normal." The religion that I had been part of for fifty-nine years was of little assistance. I was told over and over that there were no answers.

My beautiful twenty-one-year-old daughter was gone.

How could there not be an answer?

Something was mentioned to me at a bereavement group I had attended in the days following my loss. That one casual comment steered me in a certain direction which ultimately put me on a path that would transform my life.

At this juncture, I decided that for me to successfully deal with the balance of my life, I needed to take a close look at my beliefs and not to be afraid to question anything. When searching one's soul to find the root source of one's belief, often we need to take a look at our childhood, specifically our upbringing and family life. The year 2009 led me through an introspective journey that would ultimately take me places I never would have thought possible.

*

JEFF GARDNER
Jeff's 18-year-old daughter Cassidy
was killed by a drugged driver in 2013

The only way I still survive is by the grace of God, and with prayers from family and friends. I felt like I was in a tunnel for months. I couldn't, and still can't, stay focused on tasks at hand. I was never alone for the first two months after losing Cassidy. My wife took time off work and stayed beside me every minute of every day. Without her love and support, I never would have survived for even a day.

*

MICHAEL GERSHE
Mike was 8 weeks old when his 28-year-old mom
Barbara was killed by a drunk driver in 1970
Mike was 33 when his 33-year-old best friend John
was killed in a drunk driving crash in 2004

I was only an infant when my mother was killed by a drunk driver, so I didn't learn of her passing until I was a kid. I believe I am still surviving the aftermath, even though I am forty-six years old. Knowing that I almost died too doesn't make it any easier either, because I have survivor's guilt. I think, why am I alive and my mother is dead? It wasn't until college when I started to really think about my own morality and purpose in life.

My emotions still bounce between anger and sadness most of the time, because there will always be the question "What if it never happened?" I ask all the time. I think that people, even though I don't ask for it or want it, feel sorry for me at times because my mother was killed. While I understand it, I never want to use it as an excuse or crutch in my life. I was blessed with a great sense of humor that I've used in standup comedy and as an inspirational speaker presenting a program educating others about the dangers of drunk driving.

My expectations as my mother's son is to live a life where my mother would be proud of me. I feel I have a responsibility to make sure others don't go through what I have gone through, and it's a lot of pressure.

When I was thirty-three, I received a phone call around 8:30 a.m. on May 1, 2004, from Andy, one of my best friends from college. He said, "Gershe, Big John was in a fatal car accident."

"Andy, what are you talking about?" I replied. Hearing those words was just too shocking.

He said it again. "Gershe, Big John was in a fatal car accident." I heard him, but his words weren't getting through.

"Andy, what are you talking about?" I replied again.

He said a third time, "Gershe, Big John was in a fatal car accident." Once I realized that it wasn't a dream, or actually a nightmare, the words started to sink in.

I called John's mom right after that to make sure it wasn't a dream, and she confirmed it. I just felt numb as everything swirled around me. I called my father and Dolly, the woman who helped raised me after my mother was killed. John was like a brother to me and to everyone else who knew him. Then I did what I can only describe as a living hell: I called my four other best friends from college to let them know.

Every phone call started with, "Hey, are you sitting down? No? Oh, sit down. Oh, you're driving. Well, pull over."

Not only did I have to call Brent, Bryan, Dennis and Sean, but I also called others who knew and loved Big John. The calls felt endless, and were gut-wrenching.

It was, and sometimes still is, difficult to cope because John died as the result of being drunk while behind the wheel of the car. He knew that I did the program warning people about the dangers of impaired driving, and yet he died from drunk driving. I remember feeling angry, but also just lost without him.

My last phone call with Big John took place during the NFL draft when he called me, yelling about how he didn't want Kellen Winslow Jr. on his beloved team, the Cleveland Browns. Today, it remains hard to watch the draft because of that memory.

I coped by relying on friends to get me by, my humor, and yes, even a couple of visits to a therapist. People treated me very well and, of course, were sympathetic, especially those who knew him. Our college family is tight-knit, so we all just pulled together because that is what John did, he pulled us all together.

In the days after his death, I poured myself into scanning pictures and making a video of John on my computer. In that week I probably listened to Billy Joel's "Piano Man" and Styx' "Best of

Times" over a hundred times as I paired pictures with those songs. And I watched that video for weeks after. I also drove by his old apartment, just reliving memories.

*

CARL HARMS
Carl's mother Myrtle died from malpractice in 2005
Carl's 56-year-old father James was killed by a drunk driver in 2007

I felt denial and disgust in the new world I was introduced to. Along with that came depression and isolation. Unable to relax or sleep, I continued my days reluctantly. I spent a lot of time searching for answers online. In the beginning, my family understood and provided comfort, but as the hours and days passed, they became distant from my pain. I did not want to leave my home, and became very frustrated with anyone who smiled, laughed, or simply spoke in a joyous tone. I was facing a new world, and it felt far from the reality I knew. So many deaths from irresponsible people taking risks not only with their lives, but also risking lives of the innocent.

In the immediate aftermath, I didn't want to live in the new world; all I wanted was my life back. To this day, I continue to have images of my father's last moments, what he had seen, what he had felt. Coping was not in my thoughts, because this was a nightmare that I could never wake from. I became very focused on justice and answers; it seemed to be the one way I could hold onto my father, and he was still in my life.

*

STEPHEN HOCHHAUS
Stephen's 51-year-old wife Kathy
died from adult soft tissue sarcoma in 2011

My wife and I lived alone and I can only describe those first weeks and months as being in a state of shock. I did not have long to see the end coming, for I had always believed we would beat this cancer. I recall how I was walking around numb and in disbelief, yet in my own mind I felt I could handle things, for I was "a man and supposed to be strong." I denied my vulnerability. This existence went on for two and a half months until I finally broke down, ending up on the kitchen floor.

I could not have been more wrong about my vulnerability.

*

DAVID JONES
David's 54-year-old wife Judy
was killed by a drunk driver in 2008

When a family member dies due to the actions of another, there is an entirely different dimension to death. First you need to wait for the autopsy to be completed. In Judy's case, it took four and a half months before the coroner's report was completed with a finding of vehicular homicide. Then you meet with the prosecutor, followed by a grand jury deciding on which charges to present. The trial can take anywhere from a few months to years. We were lucky; there were no continuations for the thirty-seven-year-old woman charged in Judy's death, and she chose to take the plea bargain agreement.

What was unusual was that while the defense attorney asked for three years, and the prosecution asked for five years, but the judge ended up giving the driver eight and a half years based on her pattern of incidents over the past seven years.

*

JOHN PETE
John's 71-year-old grandmother Tita died
from diabetes and a series of strokes in 1989

The first several months following my grandmother's death were especially difficult. Accepting that I would never see my grandmother again in this life hit me in surges, and sometimes became quite overwhelming. The loss and grief was not just a passing event in my life, it was a very real part of everywhere I was and everything I was doing. I began to feel as if there was a kind of hopelessness and lack of purpose attached to whatever I was doing, and to life in general. When someone is suddenly gone from your life forever you begin to ask, "What's the point of anything?"

*

ROBERT RIECK
Robert's 18-year-old daughter
Ashley died by suicide in 2016

The first few weeks were really rough, as it did not seem possible that my eighteen-year-old daughter would no longer be part of our daily lives. I coped by doing a bathroom remodeling to get my mind off the reality of what had just happened.

*

CHAPTER THREE

THE FUNERAL

The song is ended, but the melody lingers on.
-IRVING BERLIN

For many, the funeral represents the end at the same time it marks a new beginning. Regardless of whether we plan a cremation and private remembrance or full burial with all the pomp, planning some type of service in the aftermath presents emotionally laden challenges. How do we get through it?

*

CHUCK ANDREAS
Chuck's 60-year-old wife Gloria
died unexpectedly from heart disease in 2014

We had a memorial service at the funeral home. I was asked by the pastor if I wanted to speak. I said I didn't think I could because of my emotional state. He said he would give me the opportunity and if I wanted to I could. The ceremony came and I was in a trance like fog. I did my best not to show emotion because I'm the man of the family. I honestly do not remember the whole ceremony. I could not get up and speak. I now wish I had, but there was no way that I could have at that time. I was very lucky that my stepdaughter

Alecia and my brother-in-law Ed were with me throughout the whole funeral home process. If not for them I could never have made all those decisions, being in the mental state I was in. Gloria and Alecia had that special mother-daughter bond where they discussed everything. I was unaware that Glor wanted to be cremated, because it was not something we had discussed. I know I said it already, but having Alecia and Ed there helping make decisions was so important, because of Glor's unexpected death and then having to do everything in such a short period of time was mind-boggling because she passed December 19, and everything had to be done quickly because of the Christmas holiday.

*

JEFF BALDWIN
Jeff's 20-year-old son Matthew died
in a drowning accident in 2011

I decided to have a celebration of life service for my son, with posters around the room at the funeral home showing different stages of Matthew's life. I also had one poster for all of Matt's school friends to sign and write messages; this poster went into his coffin.

*

ROBERT BOOS
Robert's 21-year-old son Kevin
was killed by a drunk driver in 2015

Just forty-eight hours after the crash I found myself back in Florida and driving with my daughter and ex-wife to an appointment with a local funeral home. This funeral home has been in southern Florida for a thousand years and I have actually been at this location for services for people I knew. Never did I think there would be a day when I would be going into this funeral home as a customer and arranging for the services for my little boy. We parked and walked up into this old mansion-looking funeral home. Very stereotypical, with the couches and curtains and that funeral smell that was oddly familiar. I really couldn't place my finger on what that smell was, but I would later figure it out. We were greeted by a somber and professional funeral director named Tommy. He was in full costume: dressed in a black suit, white shirt and black tie. He played the role very comfortably. I hated the guy instantly. Not because of anything he did or anything he said; he actually was very kind and appropriate at all times. I hated him for what he represented: the person who was going to arrange to put my son in a casket and bury him in the ground for all eternity.

Thankfully, Kevin's mom knew Tommy from school and they were able to chat about this and that and keep me out of it. I am a type A personality and always at the forefront of any conversation. But in this case, as I'm sure I was in shock, I murmured a hello, shook his hand and faded to the background. In my hands I clutched a T-shirt of Kevin's that still had his scent on it.

Tommy started talking about this and that. I heard bits about transporting and embalming, but to me it sounded more like the teacher on the Peanut's television show: "Waa waa waa waa waa." Thankfully, this visit was short; we would be back tomorrow to do the "formal arrangements." Great. I could hardly wait.

The next day we headed back to the funeral home. It was now my older son, my daughter and my ex-wife. I was still in my numb/shock mode, yet I was the one driving. Kevin's T-shirt sat on my lap as I drove. Suddenly a careless jerk suddenly cut me off, just missing my front bumper. I slammed on the brakes and my numbness swiftly moved to a boiling hot anger. I absolutely saw red and accelerated the car and went after him. My intent was to pull him out of his car and beat the crap out of him. Seriously. It took the yelling of my daughter to get me back to reality, and I gave up the chase.

Tommy had the day off, so we ended up with Patty, his sister who was another funeral director. This was a real family affair. Like her brother, she was dressed in black and had a somber yet helpful look on her face. She was very appropriate and very pleasant. I hated her too.

We ended up in a family conference room with my group that included my sister-in-law, my brother-in-law, and my mother. I had again given up my position as family leader, and sat quietly with Kevin's shirt in my lap. I was trying not to cry. I couldn't let my family, and especially my children, see me lose it. My job was to be the strongest one. Inside I was ripped apart. Thank God my brother-in-law and lifelong friend, Andy, was there. He took charge and spoke for me that day. I'm not sure what I would have done without him. Kevin's mom was across the table from me, dutifully taking notes for some reason and oblivious to the horror around us. I think it was her version of shock. Patty started talking. Something about standard packages and burial plots and such.

"Would you like him buried or cremated?"

Hmmm...let's see. My beautiful and wonderful twenty-one-year-old son. Would I rather have him burned to ashes and ground up by a machine, or sealed in a box in a concrete vault and buried in the ground? Who thinks about this kind of thing? When would anyone have a conversation with his child about how he or she wants their dead body treated? I said, "I have no idea." We ended up deciding to bury him in a plot my mom had.

"Would you like a viewing?"

This is such a difficult question. I remember funerals of people I have known, and when someone brings up their names (and they had a viewing), what is the image that pops into my head first? A great laugh we had at a party, or maybe a great time we had dining out? No, the image in my head is the person lying dead in a casket.

"Oh, they did such a nice job on him."

"Oh, he looks so peaceful."

I hate that. Now this was my son who people were going to have this same conversation about. But everyone else wanted a viewing, so I swallowed this bile and allowed the discussion to continue.

"What day or evening should we have the viewing and services?"

Well, this is complicated because Kevin was killed along with friends Vincenzo and Morgan. Many of the attendees would be going to all three services. We found out that Morgan's service was scheduled for a certain day and Vincenzo's was the next, so we fell in line and planned our service for the last day. Some of their friends got to dress up three times to go see a dead friend. What a lovely week.

So near the end of this torture, Patty announced that we needed to go next door to the showroom and pick out a casket. I had previously been warned from my friend Rob, Vincenzo's dad, about the "death" room. They were there earlier that day (same funeral home) and had already done all of this.

I couldn't do it. I couldn't bring myself to go pick out a box to bury my Kevin in. It was probably my primary responsibility, but I couldn't do it. I saw most of the group file out and go across the hall to the death room. I looked across the table and my daughter

Shannon was sitting there looking at me with her reddened but beautiful green eyes. I could see she was having the same issues.

A few minutes later we dared to walk together into the death room. It was full of caskets and urns and tributes. It was as horrible as it sounds. Shannon and I looked at urns, knowing we weren't using one. We stayed at the exact opposite side of the room from where the rest of the family was looking through caskets like they were in a new car showroom. Someone from the group bounded over and announced they had found one.

"Fine with me," I said.

"Don't you want to see it?"

"No."

So after a few more minutes of torture we were on our way. We had successfully completed the final arrangements for Kevin.

The next day we got the phone call saying that his body had made its way from Tallahassee and was at the funeral home. I wanted to see him. Immediately. There was something about not seeing him yet that left me some doubt that he was really gone. This could still be a horrible mistake.

Patty told us that he wouldn't be ready for a day or two. Wouldn't be ready? What did that mean? "He had been hit broadside by a driver going a hundred miles an hour and there was a lot of damage. Come to the funeral home tomorrow afternoon and he should be ready to view," she said.

So my girlfriend, Michelle, and I arrived at the funeral home shortly after noon. We had stopped at a sporting goods store and bought a brand-new Miami Dolphins jersey for Kevin to wear. Joy, Kevin's mom, and her husband Stephen came by shortly afterward.

Patty told us that they were still working on him and it would be a little while. Did we want them to call us when he was ready? We live over thirty minutes away, so we said we would wait. Joy and Stephen went to get coffee while we sat on a couch up front. I asked to speak with the technician who was handling my son.

Carl came out, and despite what he has to do for a living, he seemed like a very nice and normal kind of fellow. He explained that he was looking at the pictures we gave him and trying to match what my son looked like. He also asked if we could get a long-sleeved shirt, as his right arm was so badly damaged that it had to be concealed. So after the shock of hearing this, we went back to the same sporting goods store and bought a long-sleeved matching shirt to go under the jersey.

By the time we got back, we were informed that Kevin was ready to view.

"Do you want to go see him?"

I thought for a second and then said we needed to call my mother, brother, and Joy's sisters to get them here. It seemed only appropriate that we should all go in together.

After thirty minutes or so everyone was there and we told Patty we were ready. We were marched down a hallway to a small room. I was the last one in the line as I saw them all file into this little room. Out of the corner of my eye I saw the edge of a brown casket. I suddenly knew that inside that room was my poor Kevin lying in that box. Suddenly my legs stopped moving. I froze in place and couldn't go any farther. I was just outside the room but couldn't see anything.

I was braced for what Carl the Casket Guy had said. He told me that he had done the best he could, but Kevin was so badly bruised and injured. I pictured Dr. Frankenstein. I pictured horrible things. I couldn't go in that room.

Finally Andy came out of the room. "It's okay, Bob. He looks okay," he said gently, and took my arm. "It's okay."

It took everything I had to walk into that room. I averted my eyes and sat on a couch on the opposite side of the room. I looked at faces around the room and they all seemed sad and upset, but nobody was freaking out. Not yet, anyway. I finally turned my head and held my breath to have my first look at my son. I braced myself for the potential horror.

"I did the best I could.....," I could hear Casket Carl say.

And then I saw the familiar brown hair and very perfect beard my son had. He was so proud of that beard. I looked at his face. And his arms folded in front of him. He was sleeping. But it was him. He really was gone. I finally worked up the courage to go up to him. I remember from my grandmother's funeral ten years earlier how surprising it is how cold the skin of a deceased person is—or how hard their features are. I was careful not to touch his skin directly and instead touched the hair on his head, which felt quite normal. I dared to touch his hand, and despite being cooler than normal it did not seem as cold as I had worried about. Again, it looked like he was sleeping.

The vision of your child deceased and lying in a casket is a game-changer. Life as you knew it before, on all levels, is over. This will always be in the back of your mind. There was a very small sliver of peace after seeing him that day, because I actually saw him and knew it was him. He looked like himself. He looked "peaceful." I hate it when people say that.

The next day was the start of this horrible gauntlet of grief and suffering for three families and thousands of friends.

Day one was Morgan's wake and burial.

Day two was Vincenzo's viewing.

Day three was Vincenzo's funeral and burial, and then Kevin's wake.

Day four (Sunday) was Kevin's burial. The opening day of NFL football, which would be a huge day for all three of our children. Kevin and Vincenzo *loved* football, and since Morgan loved Vincenzo, she loved football as well.

We walked into the main hall of the funeral home on Saturday afternoon. There was that smell again, only stronger. And there, at the front of this long room, was Kevin lying in his casket waiting for everyone to come see him.

Since I was going to speak at his service the next day, I thought that since we had a four-hour wake, I would get some quiet time to reflect and think about what I wanted to talk about the next day. But that didn't happen. Over seven hundred people file into that funeral home to pay their respects. I saw people I hadn't seen in ten or twenty years. Worlds collided. Ex-wives and husbands who hadn't seen each other following a hostile divorce were there. Ex-friends of mine whom I hadn't talked to in years were there. People I worked with had come from thousands of miles away to pay their respects. If this wasn't so horrible, it would be kind of sweet.

My quiet time to reflect and write a speech to my son quickly came and went. It went from being 3 p.m. to being 7 p.m. and we were ready to start the service. I asked Andy to lead the service, as he was a minister in his church. I had also asked my friend Israel (also a minister) to speak. They were amazing. My older son Jeffrey did an amazing tribute video to his brother that brought the house down. It was sad, but it was all my Kevin. It was silly and funny and a perfect tribute to him. My friend Shelly was a tattooed little Jewish guy with long platinum hair who loved Kevin like a son. He gave a warm and funny tribute. Joy told stories about Kevin and his love affair with mustard. Shannon gave a very sweet and yet devastating tribute to her "twin" brother.

And then, it was my turn.

I was the last to speak, and I wanted to give a perfect tribute. We wanted it to be a celebration of his life, and a celebration of Kevin. The kid didn't have an enemy in the world and never met a person he didn't like. I told the story of one of the first nights after I got home to Florida, probably a night after planning the funeral and attending a candlelight service. Needless to say, I was probably exhausted and not in the best of moods. We parked our car in the neighbor's spot since they had moved out and the place was vacant. As soon as I turned off the car, I saw the security guard in his golf cart speeding toward me. I know this guy, and he wasn't the friendliest or most affable person I've ever met. He was coming to give me a hard time about parking in the neighbor's space. He really, really didn't want to mess with me right now. I was actually afraid of how I might react.

"Excuse me, sir?" he asked as he pulled up behind my car.

Deep breath. He doesn't know, Bob.

"Yes?"

"Are you Kevin's father?" he asked very gently. Where was this going?

"Yes I am."

"I just had to come over and tell you how very sorry I am for

58

your loss. Kevin was just the nicest kid. He would always stop at the guardhouse when coming in from work at night and say hello. He brought me doughnuts once. You see so many younger kids who are rude and do not even give you the time of day, and he always took the time to say hello to me. I'm going to miss him." I was stunned. I was gearing for an argument in my beaten-down state, and here I get this stunning tribute from an otherwise rather salty guy. Kevin brought the mean security guard doughnuts?

I had heard during that week that our mail delivery lady had wanted to talk to me. She had done the route for a while and was actually a coworker of Rob's. She knew Kevin and had to tell me something. Finally one afternoon I saw her putting the mail in the boxes. She saw me pull up, stopped and walked over to me, hugged me and told me how sorry she was.

"Your son was so special. He would come out and talk to me when I was putting up the mail—not like he wanted anything, he just was being friendly. On a couple of hot days he would even bring me out a cold bottled water. What a special young man."

I always knew Kevin was a caring and empathetic person, but I didn't know to the deeper level of what an amazing soul he was. I talked about how most of his life he looked up to me; he always wanted to be like me.

Now I would spend the rest of my life trying to be like him.

*

RODNEY CLOUTIER
Rodney's 21-year-old fiancéee Cattie was killed by a drunk driver in 2013, and his premature daughter Dottie died in 2016

Due to my being so far away from my fiancée, I wasn't able to be part of her funeral. This was a personal decision on my part.

For my daughter, Dottie, we had her cremated. We chose her urn. My wife didn't want a service, but I forced her into it. Hate me all you want, but four other women said it needs to happen—for closure. We had a small service, just some friends and family. Didn't want it too big.

*

M.G. COY
Myrton's 56-year-old wife Maureen
died of heart failure in 2012

Maureen's family joined me in the funeral meeting. My wife did not want a big production for her funeral, so I tried to keep it simple, but to no avail. A one-time open showing, then a church service before she was cremated. She wanted simple, but it was just a little more, mostly for her family. Our daughter gave a great eulogy at the church.

I was in a fog most of the time.

*

BILL DOWNS
Bill's 21-year-old son Brad and 19-year-old daughter-in-law
Samantha were killed by a drunk driver in 2007

When Julie and I realized we had to prepare for a funeral, we got together with Samantha's mother and family, and together we planned the funeral service. We allowed our family to attend the viewing of Brad but out of respect for Samantha's family, we left her casket closed.

Samantha's family wanted to have a separate viewing due to the size of the families, but the funeral service would still be open to the public and the caskets would be closed. Julie and I, along with Samantha's mother, made the decision that it would be better to have a closed casket service due to the physical trauma of the kids' death. Chris' mother chose to have Chris cremated instead of a casket service. This was totally out of my control, so at Brad and Samantha's service there was a portrait of Chris between their caskets.

As we prepared for the funeral and made all the arrangements, we did so in shock. We still were dealing with the fact that our kids had been murdered by an impaired driver. We had taken out insurance on Brad to keep his car insurance low, so we were able to use this to pay for the services we were planning. My thoughts were to make sure that both Samantha's family and Julie and I were happy with the arrangements we were making. This is something no parent should have to be doing and preparing for.

After the services both families agreed that the arrangements were exactly what we had planned and we had achieved our goal to honor the memory of our kids.

*

JAMES FENNELL
James' 21-year-old daughter Lauren
was killed by a drunk driver in 2008

Things you do immediately following the loss of a child are things that you never would imagine one would do in a lifetime. A cemetery plot needed to be purchased. Flowers, a casket, prayers, all needed to be decided upon. All things that are done for older people, parents, even spouses, one never imagined he would be doing for his child. Try to imagine picking a dress for your child to be buried in.

The funeral mass was special. Lauren's casket was covered with an all-white shawl. All her friends wore pink, including the guys, as a remembrance to Lauren and her love of the color. The church was packed. As we were driven from the funeral home to the church, nearly all the parking spaces in this large lot were filled. Over the years, I have noticed that funerals for the young are usually always crowded. Those for the elderly are usually sparsely attended, perhaps due to the dying off of one's friends and family or the shrinking of social circles as we become older and perhaps more withdrawn.

The ensuing procession stretched out for over a mile. And in a matter of minutes everything was over; that is, everything except dealing with the balance of one's life after such a loss.

Grieving after a child's death is a long, arduous journey. It is, however, a necessary passage. It is the letting go of sorrow. Our minds will not let us experience the depths of our grief all at once, for it would literally come close to killing us. In the beginning it comes to us in waves. The calm between the waves is short and the waves are immense. In time the waves will lessen and the calm between the waves will lengthen. There is nothing like the first months of grief following the loss of a child. I can remember a well-meaning parent telling me that the second year is worse! How could anything be worse than this? I did not realize at the time that parents feeling the same or worse in ensuing years were going around grief. To quote psychic/medium John Edward, one needs to go through grief and not around it.

It was at this point when I realized that there are very few, if any people, including professionals, who are adequately prepared or knowledgeable enough to help with this trauma. I have also come to realize that how children are lost is unimportant. What is important is the loss itself. Parents expect to see their children grow and mature. Ultimately, parents expect to die and leave their children behind. This is the natural course of life events, the life cycle continuing as it should. Losing a parent, losing a spouse, losing a sibling all are terrible losses. However, one expects to survive our parents, and perhaps even with our siblings or spouses we usually can anticipate the possibility of their loss before ours. But never our children. It has been said that when you lose your child, you lose your future.

*

JEFF GARDNER
Jeff's 18-year-old daughter Cassidy
was killed by a drugged driver in 2013

We gave Cassidy a traditional funeral. The visitation was on Thursday evening; the love and support was unbelievable. She had so many friends who came. It was very touching to see all the lives Cassidy had touched in her very short eighteen years. Trion High School students decorated her casket and showed so much support to our family. They even made Cassidy a big "T" with flowers to go on her final resting spot in the cemetery beside the school. Her aunt Autumn sang "You Are the Wind Beneath My Wings." My cousin Derrick sang "I Can Only Imagine," and the song "Butterfly Kisses" was also played. There were so many people there that you could hardly move. As we rode in the car to the burial site, I looked at the sky and saw the most beautiful rainbow.

*

MICHAEL GERSHE
Mike was 8 weeks old when his 28-year-old mom
Barbara was killed by a drunk driver in 1970
Mike was 33 when his 33-year-old best friend John
was killed in a drunk driving crash in 2004

Because I was only an infant when my mother was killed, I had no role in her funeral or memorial service. The first time I visited her in the cemetery was when my grandfather passed away when I was twenty-four.

For John's funeral, his mom, sister and brother handled the arrangements for the wake and funeral. She did ask me, along with friends Bryan, Brent, Dennis and Sean to be the pallbearers, along with anyone else who I thought would want to do it. John was six-feet four and probably over three hundred pounds when he died, so I also asked a few other close friends who I knew would do it. His brother and cousin were also pallbearers for the funeral. His mom also asked me to play host after the funeral when we had a luncheon. I asked another close friend, Matt, to help out.

The wake for John was just surreal. I waited for Sean to come from Columbus, so we made it for the second viewing, and there was a long line to see John. We had all attended a small college in Ohio, but John's impact was as enormous as he was. I didn't know if I could get through the wake. I could sense people watching me to see my reaction, and of course offering support to all of us. After I saw John lying there in the coffin with his Ashland University orientation jacket, I went outside and sat down. I needed air, I needed to process that I had just seen my friend in a coffin. Sean, who had been the closest to John, found me outside sitting on the steps. We talked for a bit and he encouraged me to go back inside. As the line went down, I had a chance to see John again. This time, one of his college roommates, Melissa, was there. As we stood there looking at him, she said, "He looks like he is sleeping." Without missing a beat, I said, "Nah, because then he would be snoring as usual." At least that got a giggle out of her. I'll never forget leaving the funeral home and seeing John's brother sitting alone in a room with his head hung low like a man lost. I wanted to go in and give him my support, but I also felt he just wanted to be left alone.

On the morning of the funeral service, after I had spent days working on the video, I forgot it at home! I was about two miles from home when I realized it and quickly turned around. We had a final chance to see Big John, and as I left the room I collapsed, and Brent held me up. It finally hit me that John was dead and I would never see him again. The emotion that I was holding in all week rushed out of me all at once.

When it was time to put John into the hearse, we all just looked at each other and said, "One, two, three, LIFT!" Even during this time, we were able to use humor to help us get by.

Wheeling John into the church and having so many eyes on us is something I hope never to do again for a long, long time. I just stared at the back of the head of whomever was in front of me to stop me from crying. It was a beautiful service, and I remember almost bursting out in laughter because Dennis dropped his program. As he reached down to get it, he gave me and Bryan one of his smiles, and it almost made me laugh. That probably wouldn't have been good, as we were sitting in the front row.

When it was time to have the luncheon afterward, I was anxious to show the video. The one thing about John is that he was one of the nicest guys in the world. His laughter would fill the room and his friends would do anything for him, because he would do anything for us. So when it was time to start the eulogy, I wanted to bring us all together and not make it so sad. So I asked something to the effect of "Anyone who ever gave John a meal or bought him a drink, raise your hand." And as all hands went up around the room, so did smiles. No one ever wanted John to "pay us back;" we just enjoyed his company.

I didn't want Matt and I to be the only ones talking, so I asked others if they wanted to speak as well. I thought people would, but

I failed to realize how difficult it would be for them. I confessed to John's mom that it was my fault that it took him six years to graduate from college, because I always turned off his alarm clock on the way back from swim practice, resulting in his missing class. I knew humor would be the only way I could get through the day. I wanted people, even though we were mourning, to smile and laugh at the memories that John gave us, because that is what he would have wanted.

*

CARL HARMS
Carl's mother Myrtle died from malpractice in 2005
Carl's 56-year-old father James was killed by a drunk driver in 2007

My mother had unexpectedly passed away just two years earlier, and her official memorial service had been put off. Our focus was on helping my father gather the pieces, so we had a family gathering but no official memorial service. For a long time prior to Dad's death, he spoke of his final days, saying that he wanted us to know that his wishes were to be cremated and mixed with my mother's ashes so they would be together forever. It was arranged for my father to be cremated in Gulfport, Mississippi, where the crash occurred, and his ashes placed with Mom's.

When my father was in the Navy we had many family outings at Cecil Field, Florida, and Lake Newman. Fortunately, Lake Newman, now managed by the city of Jacksonville, was still around and available for rental. It was arranged to have an official memorial for both my parents with full military honors. As the family prepared to say goodbye, my mind was still stuck in disbelief that both my parents were gone in a short two years.

My father spent twenty-four years in the Navy fighting for our freedom, and it was that same freedom that we abuse that killed him! The memorial service was very fitting for both of these beautiful souls. Folks brought items that reminded them of good times with my parents, and as we made it through the ceremony, folks were asked to share the items and the happy memories. The Naval Honor Guard provided a beautiful sendoff with a twenty-one-gun salute and Taps for my parents; I received the shells and flag in their memory. With all the beautiful words and honor given, I awoke the next day still in this strange world where people take something that was not theirs, the lives of innocent families.

*

STEPHEN HOCHHAUS
Stephen's 51-year-old wife Kathy
died from adult soft tissue sarcoma in 2011

Before her death, my wife, Kathy, asked not to have a service. She asked me to have her ashes combined with those of our beloved dog, who had died two years earlier. She asked that her ashes be taken to Hawaii, the place she most loved. I told her I would, but that my ashes would be with hers when that time came. Kathy died at 12:30 a.m. in the hospice home where I lay sleeping beside her. They told me I had to go, so later that morning I went to the funeral home to arrange things. I did that alone, but what happened next was very upsetting to me.

Kathy's father told me that she had wanted her ashes split between Alberta and Arizona. Since he was so devastated by his own loss, and I was very close to my in-laws, I agreed. My sister-in-law suggested I fill an urn with sand and take that up to Canada, which disturbed me even more, and I just couldn't do such a thing. They wanted to have a service for her with the ashes as soon as possible, which pushed me to get it done right away. I had to expedite the death certificate and book a flight to get to Calgary in time. The kind man at the funeral home separated Kathy's ashes and combined them with those from Mindy, our dog, for the half that remained with me. The urn I was to carry was made of wood for air travel, and even though I had all the papers in order, I was put in a room by the TSA while they figured out how to deal with me. That was the worst time I had experienced since her death, but it would get even worse after I got off the plane.

I was met by my brother-in-law and dropped off at the condo Kathy and I owned, and just left there. I had no food in the house and had to walk a short distance over the snow to get something that evening. I had never felt so low and sad as I did when I was picked up the next morning and taken to where the gathering was to happen. I did not know many of the people there and I felt incredibly alone. My wife's sister had placed an obituary in the paper, which was also something Kathy did not want. I let it go because I knew her parents needed that, and they were suffering in their own grief.

I left two days later feeling so incredibly empty and as if I had no control of my life. I also felt as if I had left half of myself behind.

*

DAVID JONES
David's 54-year-old wife Judy
was killed by a drunk driver in 2008

Over six hundred people came to Judy's funeral. Two weeks before she died, she had spent the week before two hundred and forty children and seventy adults leading vacation bible school at our church. This was an event requiring months of planning, and it came off perfectly and fully engaged the children. Judy's death did not affect just my family, but an entire community. It received TV coverage, primarily because she was a minister, but also because she had touched the lives of so many people. It was an event where everyone wanted to join together and mourn her loss. It truly does help when you have so many people offering support and feeling the loss of a wonderful person. I was too affected to speak at the funeral, but my oldest daughter, Anne, gave a wonderful speech about her mother, and I was amazed at how well she was able to articulate what an amazing person her mom was and how special their bond had become over the years. Judy had baptized Anne before our congregation only six months earlier, and now Anne gave back to her mother one last time.

In the two months after the funeral, members of our church took turns bring dinner over for my family and spending a few minutes talking about Judy and how much they missed her and asking how I was doing. That helped me a lot, as I discovered how many people cared for both of us, and I felt so privileged to have been part of her life.

*

JOHN PETE
John's 71-year-old grandmother Tita died
from diabetes and a series of strokes in 1989

A day before the funeral service I flew to Texas, where my grandparents lived. Because my grandmother had always loved having her hair and makeup done, my cousin and his wife and I went to the funeral home ahead of other family members to make sure these things had been taken care of for the viewing.

In retrospect, having some private time alone with my grandmother at the funeral home before the services helped me brace for the days ahead. We held Catholic services over a two-day period, and burial followed in a beautiful little country cemetery.

My brothers, cousins and I were all pallbearers. And while it was a difficult responsibility in the midst of our individual grief, it was also a great honor that I have very much appreciated participating in over the following years.

*

ROBERT RIECK
Robert's 18-year-old daughter
Ashley died by suicide in 2016

We had a traditional funeral and viewing. It was tough, but you are so rushed when it comes to all the decisions that have to be made and yet make sure it is something that Ashley would have wanted. My wife and I made all the decisions with the input of some other family members, as we were so overwhelmed.

*

CHAPTER FOUR

THE TRANSITION

The bereaved need more than just the space to grieve the loss. They also need the space to grieve the transition. -LYNDA CHELDELIN FELL

As we begin the transition of facing life without our loved one, some find comfort by immediately returning to a familiar routine, while others seek solitude. But the one commonality we're all faced with is determining the starting point that marks the transition from our old life to the new.

*

CHUCK ANDREAS
Chuck's 60-year-old wife Gloria
died unexpectedly from heart disease in 2014

I didn't stay away from work long, only about two weeks. It was hard staying home, because I'd just stare at the walls or the TV set. So I thought going back to work would help keep me distracted. When I first returned to work, seeing coworkers and people I knew was nice, but it was also very emotional with everyone expressing their condolences and really being so nice, but I couldn't escape the emotions, so I often left early. Working second shift was not as easy as it had been because I was getting out at 1 a.m., which in the past was perfect because I could sleep in. Now I would get home at 1 a.m. and be all alone with no one to talk to if I wanted to talk, so it was actually making things worse. The opportunity came to go to dayshift, so I talked to my sister Kim and Alecia and they agreed that trying days actually might be better, and it was, because now if I need to talk to somebody I can.

*

JEFF BALDWIN
Jeff's 20-year-old son Matthew died
in a drowning accident in 2011

I remember taking a leave of absence from work because one week, which led to two weeks, was simply not enough time. I went through every emotion that a person can go through in the weeks and months after losing Matthew. At some point I took it upon myself to try art therapy. I bought many canvases and paint, and I spent hours at a time just painting because it helped me stay busy and not be obsessed with my emotions. Trust me, I did enough crying and suffering. I found painting to be therapeutic in some kind of way. I actually ended up painting from late 2011 until early 2013. This resulted in over two hundred and thirty canvases, most of which are stored away. I have about fifteen canvases on the walls throughout my home. They bring some kind of peace when I look at them, and they also remind me of why I did them in the first place. A lot of sweat and tears went into those paintings.

*

ROBERT BOOS
Robert's 21-year-old son Kevin
was killed by a drunk driver in 2015

Exactly two weeks after the crash I returned to work. I wasn't ready to return, but since I was responsible for a huge operation, my corporate representatives were getting nervous because I wasn't coming back soon enough. Despite the support from all of them during this horrible two weeks, I felt pushed to go back to work. I should have taken more time to go back.

My first week back was like being in a dream that I couldn't wake up from. I drove to my office and went into the building hoping nobody would see me. I ran into my office, closed the door, and tried to breathe. I thought, I'm going to have to make this work somehow. Fortunately, my fellow leadership had prepped the staff (over two hundred of them) to give me space and not feel like they had to come see me on the first day. That helped a lot as I was able to gradually insert myself back into my work life.

We had a staff meeting on the Thursday I got back, which I normally lead. I had two hundred sets of expectant eyes watching my every move in our auditorium. I got through it, being business all the way until the very end. I told them, as they knew, that the past couple of weeks had been horrible but that their good wishes and thoughts had meant the world to my family. I couldn't thank them enough. As soon as I was done talking, I ran into my office so I didn't have to talk to anyone. I usually stay afterward and chitchat with most of them and ask how they are doing. I just couldn't do that on that day.

In the long run, work was therapeutic. Being as busy as I am from day to day helped a lot. A busy mind did not have me dwelling on the loss of my son. It was only in the quiet moments that I would fall into that deep sorrow, so I tried to avoid it as much as possible.

*

RODNEY CLOUTIER
Rodney's 21-year-old fiancéee Cattie was killed by a drunk
driver in 2013, and his premature daughter Dottie died in 2016

When my fiancée passed away, I took the next day off. The day after that I had a mandatory safety meeting which I ended up leaving halfway through because it was about rollovers. Cattie had died in a rollover accident.

As for my daughter, two days after we came home from the hospital I finally got a job offer. I had been unemployed for almost six months at that time. Chelsea told me to go, that we need the job.

*

M.G. COY
Myrton's 56-year-old wife Maureen
died of heart failure in 2012

I worked part time, four hours in morning. It took a month before I returned to work. I started therapy after my doctor recommended it. This was a new experience, one I had no knowledge of. I had spent thirty-five years with a person who had loved me, unconditional love. I had a very hard time finding reading material to help men deal with this problem. Out of twenty-eight books, only six were for men.

*

BILL DOWNS
Bill's 21-year-old son Brad and 19-year-old daughter-in-law
Samantha were killed by a drunk driver in 2007

I returned to work seventy days after the death of our kids. Being in maintenance, there were many times that I was working alone, which gave me plenty of time to contemplate the death of the kids. The regrets, the grief and memories were overwhelming. My work was hampered by the grief I was feeling. The emotion that would take over my thoughts would cause me to have panic attacks and leave me an emotional wreck. I often took off from work, or not even go to work because I just could not handle long hours of my mind being idle, remembering the kids' demise.

My fellow employees did not know how to handle my emotional outbursts or lack of being social. I would often just go to a boiler room at one of the schools where I performed maintenance and find a place to hide out to avoid people and the kids in the school. I tried to stay busy with my job to keep my mind busy, but I always found myself in an emotional meltdown. Just when I thought I was doing better, I would run into someone who knew the kids and have to respond to someone acknowledging they were gone, and again would spiral into an emotional meltdown.

Eventually when school was out for the summer, it became easier to hide the meltdowns because there were no one there who I had to hide from. I began the summer maintenance, and was able to maintain a busy mind and think of my work—and bury my grief deeper.

*

JAMES FENNELL
James' 21-year-old daughter Lauren
was killed by a drunk driver in 2008

Some parents who have lost a child find it difficult to return to work. The thought of returning to work is incomprehensible to some. For others, who might be the breadwinner for a family still dependent upon them, there is no choice.

I owned my own business when I lost my daughter, and I can honestly say that returning to work was the best possible thing for me. It helped keep my mind active, and although the loss never left my conscious mind, not even for an instant, working did help me start to reclaim my life.

The challenges of running an active business, along with weekly buying trips out of state and trying to care for my mom's needs, kept me from dwelling on my situation. The evenings, when facing the quiet and solitude of the night, were when my new journey would be extremely difficult. On days I was home, driving past the schools that Lauren had attended, the places she liked to shop, her places of employment, and, yes, the places I would meet her in the wee hours of the morning when she would run out of gas, proved to be painful.

*

JEFF GARDNER
Jeff's 18-year-old daughter Cassidy
was killed by a drugged driver in 2013

I returned to work after eleven weeks off. The company I worked for was so very supportive in my time of need. I had been diagnosed with post-traumatic stress disorder while I was off work, and they helped me get on short-term disability. I was so scared to go back the first day of work. I knew everyone would be looking at me and offering condolences. I didn't know how I would respond. Some days I would be all right. Some days I would think of Cassidy and break down and have to go home. After six months I had to quit my job. I just couldn't handle the stress of the environment anymore. I returned to my previous (and current) employer. I work there with a great friend who knows my situation and understands.

*

MICHAEL GERSHE
Mike was 8 weeks old when his 28-year-old mom
Barbara was killed by a drunk driver in 1970
Mike was 33 when his 33-year-old best friend John
was killed in a drunk driving crash in 2004

I grew up without my mother, so in a way it was just a normal life without her. I had no issues with school as a kid other than the usual "not paying attention" reports that I got. I recall always writing "deceased" on any school forms when they asked for my mother's name. The effects of her death really didn't impact me until I was able to fully comprehend what it all meant when I was in high school and college.

I was a collegiate swimmer, so I used swimming as a distraction as I thought about my mother, the car crash, and my own existence. It definitely helped, because I would swim while angry in practice and in meets. I'm not saying it helped me win the races, but it was the only time when I could really just be alone in my thoughts. I was a distance swimmer, and when you're swimming a mile you have lots of time to think.

When John died 2004, I remember going into work at Kent State University, where John also worked, but in the athletic department. My coworkers all knew John very well, and offered their incredible support. My direct supervisor allowed me to take the week off, and I think it was mostly due to his knowing John. I was very lucky to have such support in that office. I do recall being unfocused at work when I did return. I don't believe grieving for John hurt my work habits. If anything, it helped me recover better because of all the people who knew and cared for John.

*

CARL HARMS
Carl's mother Myrtle died from malpractice in 2005
Carl's 56-year-old father James was killed by a drunk driver in 2007

My family grew very frustrated with me because I wouldn't simply move on, and my number one priority was making sure my father's death wasn't unnoticed and someone answered for it. I spent three years at home on the computer late at night researching these tragedies and networking through MySpace social media. This was the one place where I found folks who understood, folks who had an experience similar to mine. Along with that, when I did leave my house it was to travel from Jacksonville to Mississippi for court. I wanted answers, I wanted to know why it happened when there was no logical answer. Suffering, I reached out to different advocacy groups but was let down by the support I didn't receive until I found the family I could count on, which accepted my fears, my darkness and my need for answers. Ultimately, through state training, it took me three years, and I went to work with that same agency and became a homicide victim advocate.

*

STEPHEN HOCHHAUS
Stephen's 51-year-old wife Kathy
died from adult soft tissue sarcoma in 2011

As I owned my own business and had missed so much time

being with Kathy, and also on the trip to Canada, I had to be at work the very day she died. The funeral home was just down the street, so I was waiting for it to open. Winter is our busiest time of the year, and I needed to keep my income alive. Although I knew I could have stayed home, I just thought it would be filled with sorrow. I felt that having people around me might make things more bearable. I worked as best I could but went into the bathroom frequently because I kept losing control. I didn't want anyone to see me crying. My sister came to stay with me and had she not, I don't know how I could have made it through the nights of the first week. As the months went by I worked long hours to try to recover financially. I think it was also to keep my mind busy, although I still am not certain that worked very well.

*

DAVID JONES
David's 54-year-old wife Judy
was killed by a drunk driver in 2008

When Judy died, I also died. She had been such an integral part of my life that I felt as if my life had gone from color to black and white. My body lived, but my life would never have the same richness and beauty that it had before that fateful day in August. When you lose your life partner, it physically hurts. It is as if someone socked you in the stomach and you feel a sense of unease and tension all the time. For me it was as if I was in two worlds: one where Judy still lived and I was expecting her to walk through the door any minute, and one where she was gone and I was alone. I could rationalize everything, but emotionally I felt as if part of me had died.

The body does go on, and gradually the constant tension ebbs and flows, so that at times you relax and forget. For me, the best thing was taking walks in the woods and seeing beautiful settings of nature to appreciate God and how he works in our lives. I drove with my son Michael out to Missoula, Montana, a week after the funeral as he returned to school at the University of Montana and I soaked up the scenery. We took a day trip to Glacier National Park just before classes started, and I can remember the majestic snow-capped mountains and sweeping panoramic views and feeling that God was at work.

I visited the cemetery every day and sometimes met others who had loved ones buried near Judy's grave; we shared each other's stories. We all had plots next to our loved ones, so we would be future neighbors for eternity, and that gave us a bond. One woman's husband had been a police officer directing traffic on a dark rainy night when he was killed by a hit-and-run driver. Eventually the girlfriend of the man who killed him ratted him out to the police after he abandoned her, but it was not admissible as evidence. The police did surveillance and eventually arrested him for drug dealing, and he was sentenced to prison.

Another woman visited the grave next to Judy's, and I asked why she had not put up a headstone. She said it was because she could not decide if she wanted to leave her husband buried there or move him to a different cemetery. She died six months later and now she and her husband have a headstone next to Judy's. I realized how short our lives truly are and that our time is but the blink of any eye to God; some are just longer than others.

When I compare the dates on the headstones, many are shorter than Judy's, the saddest being those of children. I wondered how they had died and how their parents were coping. Even now, each time someone new is buried, I often find out about that person and his or her life, and feel strongly that we all have souls that live on afterward and that some day I will see Judy again.

*

JOHN PETE
John's 71-year-old grandmother Tita died
from diabetes and a series of strokes in 1989

Upon flying home after my grandmother's burial, I felt a need to get back to familiar routines. But I found that returning to work was both a blessing and a curse while coping with my loss.

Work was generally a very helpful distraction, but there were also times when painful grief surfaced during the work day and made it difficult to concentrate and get through the day. But somehow you dig deep and weather those first weeks back at work, and you gradually adjust to your loss and how life is forever changed.

*

ROBERT RIECK
Robert's 18-year-old daughter
Ashley died by suicide in 2016

I believe my wife and I took about two weeks to get ourselves back to some sort of balance. My owning a couple of businesses made it hard to be in the customer service field, as I really did not want all the questions, etc., about her death.

*

SMILE WHEN YOU THINK ABOUT ME

BY JEFF BALDWIN
February 4, 2014

Our time together on earth was just the beginning. Although I am not there in the physical sense, I see you clearly. I see the pain that you're going through and I realize just how much you love me.

But don't mourn me for too long. Turn your sadness into smiles. Think about the special moments we shared together; you know the times. I remember them all because they are locked away right here in my heart.

We will be together again. I will see you clearly and you will see me the same. We were not put on earth to stay for very long. Some of us leave young while others live to be very old, but we all must take that same passage someday.

And fear not, for I will be right there waiting when it is your time to take that walk. Hand in hand, we will go into the promise land and there we will live forever.

There is no pain here; no sadness nor tears. We all stay busy and we all are on different levels. We can think of something and be there in the moment. Like when I see you crying, I am right there beside you. We have a love that will never end. I learned so much from what you instilled in me, and although I didn't always listen at the time, I now know you did it because you loved me, so wipe those tears and smile for me.

I won't be far. Although you cannot see me, know in your heart that I have not left you. I am just in heaven with God and all my other family members; some you told me about and others that I have come to know since I have been here. If you could see what I see, you would really be smiling. I am in no pain, only happiness. And we still learn so many things in heaven. Some of us help others who are passing, while others help those adjust to life in heaven. Life on earth is only the beginning.

Please remember I am always with you. I hear your prayers and it makes me smile when you send love to heaven for me, because I send it right back . . .

CHAPTER FIVE

THE QUESTION

When someone you love becomes a memory, that memory becomes a treasure. -UNKNOWN

One day we have our loved one, the next day he or she is no longer here. How do we explain to others something we can't wrap our brain around? How do we answer the question "How did your loved one die?"

*

CHUCK ANDREAS
Chuck's 60-year-old wife Gloria
died unexpectedly from heart disease in 2014

I appreciate talking about Glor anytime, but I found out it's easier talking about her in a one-on-one situation rather than with a group of people. When I discuss her with a group, I find myself becoming more emotional. I truly believe that the more I talk about her, it helps to strengthen the memory of her, and that is important to me. I won't lie, and I now have a stock answer unless it's a person I feel close to. I learned a lesson early on that some people ask how you are doing and don't really mean it, just sort of a natural way to start a conversation, like "Nice weather we're having." One person asked me how I was feeling, so I started telling him, and he rolled his eyes. Of course I became mad, because I couldn't believe he did that, so I just don't open up to anyone anymore. My answer to most people is "As well as can be expected, I guess."

*

JEFF BALDWIN
Jeff's 20-year-old son Matthew died
in a drowning accident in 2011

I never miss the opportunity to bring my son's name up to others who may be meeting me for the first time or those friends who feel like it's taboo to mention my son's name. He lived and his life mattered, and I like to share the things that made my son unique in his own way with everyone who will listen to me. Even though it's been five years since my son drowned, I don't like the word "died." Perhaps I am still guarding my heart in some strange way; however, I always use the word "passed," because to me passed means to transition from this life into the next, which is heaven for me. I feel like friends avoid the subject of bringing up our child who has died because they feel like they are sparing us undue pain, which I respect, because deep down I feel that people genuinely don't know what to say in situations like that.

*

ROBERT BOOS
Robert's 21-year-old son Kevin
was killed by a drunk driver in 2015

As a leader of a large business organization, I am often confronted by the small talk of other businesses, salespeople, and colleagues from different states who really do not know me. Up until last year, I hadn't really thought about this. Now, as innocent and normal as it is, it becomes a game.

"So, Bob, how many children do you have?"

"Between my girlfriend and me, we have five children."

"How old are they?"

"Believe it or not, they go right in order: 25, 24, 23, 22 and 21."

"Boys or girls?"

"Two boys, three girls."

"Wow, that's amazing. Are they in school?"

Now about this time, anyone also in the meeting who works with me or knows my personal situation starts to get a look of horror on his or her face. Will this person continue to push and walk right into this discussion?

The truth is, ninety-seven percent of the time I'm usually able to run this conversation off and we get down to business. But sometimes the person is persistent.

"Two have graduated. Two are still in school. One is off doing other things."

I have actually determined that "other things" is a better way to say he's dead. Most of the questioning ends with the description above, but a couple of people have persisted. Mind you, this entire time I'm saving them from the bomb I'm going to drop on them if they really want to know. I don't mind talking about my son and what happened, and I actually find it soothing sometimes to talk about him. I'm not sure my inquisitive friends are really prepared for this. But they continue to push and continue to quiz me, and eventually I'm going to lay it on them.

"So what is the kid doing that you call it other things?"

Before I answer, have the camera pan over to my coworkers and the looks on their faces. I shrug as if to tell them I have tried to avoid this. "Well, since you are going to keep asking, here's the full reason. My son Kevin was killed by a drunk driver in September 2016. He was twenty-one years old."

If it wasn't such a tragic situation it might actually be a funny story. In a normal situation I welcome talk about my son. The issue is that most people are very uncomfortable bringing his name up to me, as though they are opening a deep wound or making me remember he is gone. Trust me, I know he's gone. I want to talk about him; I want to hear stories about him that I didn't know. I want to laugh at his antics. Sure, I might get sad thinking about it, but I will do my utmost to hide that from you so you aren't uncomfortable.

*

RODNEY CLOUTIER
Rodney's 21-year-old fiancéee Cattie was killed by a drunk
driver in 2013, and his premature daughter Dottie died in 2016

I don't get asked about my fiancée anymore. As for my daughter, there is a pause and a flashback of the moment when I cut her umbilical cord. I shed a few tears and I answer the question.

*

M.G. COY
Myrton's 56-year-old wife Maureen
died of heart failure in 2012

I talk about Maureen a lot and everyone understands my need to talk about her, and everyone says it does not bother them. In fact, I was told that if I did not, they would worry about me. No one I know has been in my difficult situation, but they try hard to understand. I am surrounded by good friends.

*

BILL DOWNS

Bill's 21-year-old son Brad and 19-year-old daughter-in-law
Samantha were killed by a drunk driver in 2007

When someone asks me how many kids I have, I always say I have two kids, one who is living and one who is deceased. Often they will then ask how the one died, and I always explain to them that Brad, along with his wife of three months, Samantha, and friend Chris, whom I also consider my son and daughter, were murdered by an impaired and distracted driver. I love to talk about my kids, whether it is my daughter Cindy, or Brad, Samantha and Chris. It gives me an opportunity to brag and remember how wonderful they are.

When they ask about Brad, Samantha and Chris, I always take the opportunity to tell them how important they are to my life even after death, and how important it is not to drive while impaired or distracted. Often the emotion makes me take a moment to breathe and reflect, but I am always so honored when someone shows genuine interest in their memories. Often when I am standing in a room full of offenders, people who have been arrested for driving while impaired or distracted, my conversation is a two-edged sword. I brag of my kids and share the memories, but I always make sure the class realizes that driving while impaired or distracted is a conscious choice, not a mistake. It is at this time when I choose what part of my testimony I want to share with them, and it depends on the class demeanor on how forceful or compassionate I am with them.

No matter where or when I talk about my kids, I always share their memories with anyone willing to listen and who is genuinely interested. Sometimes I show emotion, but it all depends on who I am talking to.

*

JAMES FENNELL
James' 21-year-old daughter Lauren
was killed by a drunk driver in 2008

I never look for an opportunity to change the subject whenever my daughter is mentioned. I have begun to realize that she has never left us. She is just in another realm. This realization came to me over time, and with each passing year became stronger and stronger. When people ask me "How many children do you have?" I always include my Lauren, and yes, I explain that she has passed on. My goal is not to make anyone uncomfortable but to include my daughter in my everyday life, as she is as much my daughter now as when she was here on earth.

*

MICHAEL GERSHE
Mike was 8 weeks old when his 28-year-old mom
Barbara was killed by a drunk driver in 1970
Mike was 33 when his 33-year-old best friend John
was killed in a drunk driving crash in 2004

When people ask about my family, for example on a first date, it can be very awkward. Even though I am used to talking about the car crash on stage during my program, telling someone who is not expecting it is very difficult. I don't want anyone to feel sorry for me when I share the fact my mother was killed when I was an infant, but I also know it's human nature to do so. It makes me uncomfortable to answer, only because I know it will shock the other person, but it's a part of my life.

Even though my mother was killed, my brother and I got lucky with a woman named Dolly who helped raise us. She was hired shortly after the car crash to look after us while my father worked.

She became our mother figure over the years, and we are her sons. The first time I can recall telling someone about my mother, I was probably in third grade. My neighbor across the street asked where my mother was. Dolly, who is Jamaican and is helping to raise two white Jewish boys, overheard him ask me the question. My initial answer was, "I will tell you later." I really didn't know how to answer, but she told me to tell him right there and then. I would like to say it's gotten easier over the years, but I would be lying. But Dolly gave me the courage to tell people.

I appreciate the opportunity to talk about my mother, especially if I know it can change or save lives when it comes to impaired driving prevention. I want my mother to be proud of me, so I think I am able to do that by telling her story.

The only time I talk about John is with others in our circle of friends, or while presenting The Magic of Life when I share what happened to him. I appreciate the opportunity to go down memory lane with my friends, but I also share who he was with an audience. Big John was full of life, and I never shy away from an opportunity to talk about him. I talk about what he meant to me, his family and his friends by sharing stories about who he was when he lived. It's important for his legacy to live on so others learn from him in regard to how he died.

*

STEPHEN HOCHHAUS
Stephen's 51-year-old wife Kathy
died from adult soft tissue sarcoma in 2011

How I answer questions about my wife varies, depending on who asks the question. If a customer comes into my store who knew Kathy and asks about her, I have a hard time telling them she has died, for they knew her and it often hurts them to hear to hear the news. That can cause me to tear up, and that's not so good. When someone in the medical, legal, or government field asks a question, I feel little emotion now, although in the first few months it was not that way.

When a close friend or family member, especially my grandchildren, asks a question about Kathy, I smile when I answer, for the love comes out and happy memories overshadow the sad ones. I could go on for hours talking about her, rarely with sorrow, though that still lingers.

*

DAVID JONES
David's 54-year-old wife Judy
was killed by a drunk driver in 2008

I love to talk about Judy whenever I have the chance. She was an incredible person and my spiritual mentor. Talking about her helps me to remember all the little things about her, and I feel that as long as I can keep a perfect image of her then she still lives, at least for me. I also look at using the questions about her as a way of maybe preventing DUI driving, even if only for a time or two.

*

JOHN PETE
John's 71-year-old grandmother Tita died
from diabetes and a series of strokes in 1989

When I lost my grandmother over twenty-five years ago, it was initially very hard to talk about. But somewhere along the way conversations began to shift from difficult and painful loss to reminiscing about the happy memories. My grandmother often shared family stories, traditions and interesting superstitions from our Hispanic heritage while I was growing up. And I still enjoy reminiscing and sharing those with others all these years later.

CHAPTER SIX

THE DATES

Grievers use a very simple calendar. Before and after. - LYNDA CHELDELIN FELL

Sadness and sorrow become part of our new routine. But among the 365 calendar dates, we can count on two of those days to bring an extra wave of sadness: our loved one's birthday and the day he or she died. How do you celebrate the life that is no more? How do you acknowledge the painful date that marks your loved one's death?

*

CHUCK ANDREAS
Chuck's 60-year-old wife Gloria
died unexpectedly from heart disease in 2014

So far I have only had to experience one birthday which actually made me think about Glor's last one. We celebrated it with Alecia and Heather and had a wonderful time, which actually made this one easier to deal with. Everyone was laughing, singing and dancing; it was just one of those memorable nights. As always, I prefer to spend these personal days alone. It is easier for me to control my emotions when I'm by myself, of course, but that's the way I've always been.

I am fortunate that my family realizes that and I know that they're there if I need them. Glor's birthday and the anniversary of her death are only a month apart. I really never had a chance to get over one before the other one was on my doorstep per se. Because they are so close, it actually went from one to the next; it was a long month. Her birthday is November 17 and her passing was on December 19, and lo and behold, there is Christmas. It was and is a trying time.

*

JEFF BALDWIN
Jeff's 20-year-old son Matthew died
in a drowning accident in 2011

Just this year, 2016, would have been my son's twenty-fifth birthday, since he left just a month after turning the Big Two O. Up until this time I have just gone through the motions on his birthday and the anniversary of his passing, or as we parents like to call it, the *angelversary*. However, this year, with it being his twenty-fifth birthday, I felt the time was finally right to celebrate it. I invited my ex-wife and her family to meet me and my friends at my son's gravesite for a balloon release at 7:30 that evening. We bought twenty-five balloons in all colors to release because my son had a thing for tennis shoes in all colors. I once called them the clown shoes, but he loved those shoes, so I suggested an assortment of different colors. I brought a CD player and I had downloaded "Dancing in the Skies." We played that song as we released the balloons with a twenty-five number countdown. The feeling was bittersweet, to say the least. I felt accomplished because I did this instead of sitting at home and crying or watching home videos of him. I decided to truly honor his life and memory. I feel that this is just the tip of the iceberg for future anniversaries. They will have to be thought out, and everyone will be welcomed like this time.

*

ROBERT BOOS
Robert's 21-year-old son Kevin
was killed by a drunk driver in 2015

My son was killed on Labor Day weekend, 2015. Just weeks after his death we endured a gauntlet of dates that made every moment worse.

Thanksgiving was in late November, just weeks after his death.

The following week was his birthday on December 6, the two-month anniversary of his death.

Two weeks later, December 20, was my birthday.

A week later was the Christmas holiday, easily the most difficult, heartbreaking and soul-wrenching time.

A week later was New Year's. We were able to bid adieu to a horrible year, 2015, and enter a new year, 2016, one that my son and his friends never saw.

The final run on this gauntlet was a backhand out of nowhere, one that you can't brace for because you didn't know it was coming. Of course, the holidays and birthdays mentioned above were indescribably horrible, but at least you braced yourself. I didn't see this one coming.

Super Bowl Sunday. This is an American holiday as much as any other day, but isn't on the calendar. Since Kevin was a huge football fan and we talked sports together almost constantly, this day hit me like a ton of bricks. I sat in the living room of a friend's house and found myself actually enjoying the game and all the commercials. This, of course, happened only for a very short time. Once I realized I was actually enjoying myself, I was awash in a wave of guilt that my son was not here to enjoy it with me. A day that started out being enjoyable ended up in a very black cloud. Of course, I am such a wonderful actor and able to hide this pain, so I'm not sure any of my friends even noticed. There was very small silver lining on Super Bowl Sunday, and it happened just as my pain was reaching its crescendo. The game was okay, but the commercials were becoming ridiculous. How many different cute animal commercials or beverage ads could we bear?

Then it happened. A public service advertisement when companies were paying millions of dollars for precious advertising space. It was Academy award-winning actress Helen Mirren. You would remember her from "The Queen" and "The Hundred-Foot Journey," among many others. She was sitting at a table with a beer. She went on to call out drunk drivers for their irresponsibility and scolded them very heavily. I couldn't believe it.

A couple of months later on an impulsive whim, I scoured the internet to find a contact for Ms. Mirren so I could send her a thank you note. Without revealing my successful path, I did find a way to send an email hoping that someday, amidst what are probably a thousand notes she receives, she would see mine and at least know how thankful and impressed I was. Imagine my surprise when the very next morning I received a personal reply from her (I have asked for and received her permission to share this with you):

Dear Mr. Boos,

I am so very, very sad to hear of the loss of your son. I cannot imagine anything more painful and more unspeakably tragic than losing your child in such a way. So many lives are profoundly affected and possibly destroyed by one person's unconscionable action taken in a state of inebriation. That action of stepping into a car and turning on the ignition.

I send you and all your family my love, my thoughts, and my deepest sympathy for your pain.

It is extremely kind of you to take the time to send an appreciation of the anti drunk driving piece. Anheuser-Busch prepared, shot, and paid for the advertising for the Super Bowl, knowing that many millions would be watching and many of them enjoying a beer. It was very responsible of them, and as you can imagine, a very expensive process. I will pass on your appreciation if you don't mind. I think it will mean a great deal to those responsible, and encourage them to do more.

With all love,

Helen Mirren

It is a note that I will keep close to my heart always. The next time you go to see a movie that has Helen in it, please remember her kindness and compassion to all those who have lost someone, and that special moment she took that meant so much to me.

*

RODNEY CLOUTIER
Rodney's 21-year-old fiancéee Cattie was killed by a drunk
driver in 2013, and his premature daughter Dottie died in 2016

I never got the chance to celebrate my financee's birthday. I do wish her a happy birthday, and "I miss you and love you" on her passing. As for my daughter, as of this moment it's been a little over three months since her birth and death. However, she was due on my birthday, July 22, and I'm not sure how it's going to go.

*

M.G. COY
Myrton's 56-year-old wife Maureen
died of heart failure in 2012

Our only daughter meets me for a lunch together. The first year her family tried to me us. But that stopped. I did start a scholarship at the high school Maureen worked at, and the recipients are very grateful. A bittersweet moment for us.

*

BILL DOWNS
Bill's 21-year-old son Brad and 19-year-old daughter-in-law
Samantha were killed by a drunk driver in 2007

Since I am a very emotional type of person, coping with the birthdays is actually easier for me than dealing with the death anniversary, which we at AVIDD like to call *angelversary*, the day our loved ones became angels. For the birthdays, we usually go out to the cemetery and wish the kids happy birthday. We spend some time remembering and celebrating their lives and what they meant to us. We reflect on how blessed we are to have had them in our lives.

For their death anniversary, or *angelversaries* the emotion is quite different than the birthdays, of course. We had started a family tradition since their deaths by going to the cemetery at the exact time they were killed, 8:52 p.m. on October 6. We did this because we were there for our son's first breath, but we were deprived of being there for his last breath. So we promised we would be there at their time of death until we take our last breath. We always light a candle in honor of each of them. So there are three candles. For the longest time, our families and a few friends went with us, but over the years it has been just Julie, our daughter Cindy, and me. Everyone else has moved on, which is not surprising. For many people who have lost loved ones, their families and friends move on and go on with their lives.

During both birthdays and angel dates we try to stay positive; however, sometimes it is not an easy thing to do. Losing a child, especially in such a horrific and horrible way is not something you ever get over. A parent who loses a child, no matter how it happens, has a really hard time going forward. It never gets easier, but you learn to fake it until you make it.

*

JAMES FENNELL
James' 21-year-old daughter Lauren
was killed by a drunk driver in 2008

I understand how balloon releases and other rituals can seem to provide comfort to parents. However, as I have progressed through understanding my own loss, I have begun to realize that they are only bandages, liniments or salves. I think once we can finally come to accept that we are *not* our physical bodies but actually inhabiting them, it becomes a little easier to grasp. In essence, we are spiritual beings embarking on a material experience and that is what we refer to as the human being. Once one comes to that realization, we start to understand that we can communicate with them on a daily basis, if we choose, and the anniversary date or birthday remembrance becomes less important. My daughter has become a part of my daily life, and I can honestly say that I feel her love now more than ever.

*

MICHAEL GERSHE
Mike was 8 weeks old when his 28-year-old mom
Barbara was killed by a drunk driver in 1970
Mike was 33 when his 33-year-old best friend John
was killed in a drunk driving crash in 2004

Coping with my mother's birthday or the anniversary of the car crash is usually depressing. In a way, it's a catch-22, because I don't have any memories, but I wish I did. I think about her birthday and it saddens me that I never had the chance to say happy birthday to my own mother. I tend to withdraw and like to be alone with my own thoughts around anniversaries. I take a personal inventory on my life and hope that my mother would be proud of me and the way I am living my life.

I know the anniversaries hit my father the hardest, and I cannot imagine what he goes through either. I think we find strength in each other around these special dates. In the Jewish tradition, we light a Yahrzeit candle in remembrance of our loved ones that burns for twenty-four hours.

Coping with John's birthday and anniversary can be quite tough for me too. I started a "Friends of Big John" Facebook page, so we tend to post pictures or stories of him, which makes it comforting for all of us. Together we support each other and that at least gives me strength to get through his anniversaries. I may also withdraw a bit around both the dates. I don't know if my friends look at me for a sign of strength, but if they do I am honored.

One year I had to present in front of DUI offenders on the anniversary of Big John's death. That was very uncomfortable because it was already an emotional day, but to stand in front of about sixty offenders and talk about him was brutal. There are times where I am still very angry with John, because he knew I was a survivor of a drunk driving crash, and that is how he died. I thought he knew better, and yet he died as the result of being the drunk driver.

As someone who lost one of his best friends, I think as a man, we honor them in a way that will make us cry, but yet laugh at some silly story, and that is what I do. I will watch the DVD that I made and remember the great times we had together. It brings me comfort, but at the same time it makes me miss that guy with the goofy smile and booming laugh.

*

STEPHEN HOCHHAUS
Stephen's 51-year-old wife Kathy
died from adult soft tissue sarcoma in 2011

My wife died in February, and the following March was to be her fifty-second birthday. I had promised her that I would take her to Palm Springs, California, after her surgery and we would go to her favorite restaurant. I chose to go on that trip alone and out to dinner regardless of how hard it would be. Somehow I felt I was honoring Kathy by doing so. Although it was hard, it was sweet as well. I ordered her favorite meal and toasted her silently, and every year it has become easier to do. I suppose I shall do so always.

The day of her death is one that holds little meaning, for it was a day I do not wish to dwell on. It has little meaning in relation to the life she lived. That day also happens to be my daughter-in-law's birthday, so by celebrating that I can more easily let go of the sadder associations.

The day of our anniversary has become quite special. I try to take a trip to one of our favorite places and go out to dinner, celebrating the day she chose to spend the rest of her life with me: no small event in my life. As it shall always be my anniversary, I will always enjoy that day. That first anniversary I was alone, and as it happened it was also the day my father died. So I can let that day go for just the same reason as Kathy's. I choose to celebrate life, not death, for even in grief I can choose to remember the happier times more than the sad. Valentine's Day was also a huge time for us, and so I go out for dinner. Even with couples all around I can still find a quiet spot in the lounge and enjoy a nice dinner, having placed a card next to her urn at home.

*

DAVID JONES
David's 54-year-old wife Judy
was killed by a drunk driver in 2008

Those days are truly difficult and are only eleven days apart. Our anniversary is the next month and is equally hard. If I am in town I visit Judy's grave and sit awhile and look at photos, read her old emails, and listen to some of her sermons. In other years I have taken long walks on the beach and contemplated the ocean and God's plan for both of us. I believe that God is using me to tell Judy's story to help save the lives of others. Sometimes I think of those unknown people who are alive today because of her. I like to think there are a few little children, and knowing Judy, she would have been pleased to know that. I will be buried next to Judy, and I've spent many hours at her grave talking to her and praying. It's a lovely site. A playground sits across the street, and I know she would have appreciated that touch. It is also next to the church where we were married nearly twenty-nine years before she died. Near her grave are two pretty oaks with a stone bench between them where I've sat for hours. When I visit, it always helps me put other problems into perspective and realize they are really not that important.

*

JOHN PETE
John's 71-year-old grandmother Tita died
from diabetes and a series of strokes in 1989

Our family doesn't generally gather on birthdays or anniversaries for lost loved ones, but I light a candle in my own home. I also often call other family members to remember and share memories. There is always a mix of sadness and happiness in remembering my grandmother and other lost loved ones, but all these years later it is much easier to remember the happy and special times we shared.

CHAPTER SEVEN

THE HOLIDAYS

The only predictable thing about grief is that it's unpredictable. -LYNDA CHELDELIN FELL

The holiday season comes around like clockwork, and for those in mourning this time of year brings a kaleidoscope of emotions. If the grief is still fresh, the holidays can be downright raw. How do we navigate such a festive season that once held the promise of magical holiday memories?

*

CHUCK ANDREAS
Chuck's 60-year-old wife Gloria
died unexpectedly from heart disease in 2014

Christmas will always be my hardest holiday because I always liked to see that special smile and emotions when I could surprise her with a present she never expected. Christmas was also the day I proposed to her, so it's always been a holiday I liked. Gloria always decorated the house, even to the point of the Christmas-themed pot holders. She always did such a fine job of decorating the tree; her attention to detail, especially because she was an upholsterer, was unbelievable. She had to have only certain bulbs on the tree that reminded her of certain Christmases and memories of people. And one thing that always had to be under the tree was Alecia's old ceramic house that lights up. I remember one year she couldn't find it right away, and the tree or Christmas wasn't complete until she found it. Needless to say, last year I didn't put up any, and I don't think I will ever decorate for Christmas again.

Glor passed away a week before Christmas. She had the house all decorated and the tree was perfect as always. I left all the decorations up for the month of January. Removing the decorations from the tree and around the house was one of the hardest things I've ever done, because I knew it would never look this way again. Another thing which makes Christmas hard is all the commercials and songs about having a merry Christmas, being with loved ones and seeing their smiling faces plastered all over the place. I used the mute button on the TV, and riding in my truck without listening to the radio happened a lot. So one of the things I have to keep reminding myself about is trying to smile and not put a damper on everyone else's holiday, because it's not their fault that this holiday is now hard for me.

*

JEFF BALDWIN
Jeff's 20-year-old son Matthew died
in a drowning accident in 2011

The holidays can be filled with triggers that can bring you down to your knees in tears. I remember that first Christmas, because I still had to go out and buy my daughters Christmas gifts. I was doing good that Saturday morning. I went to the mall first and then to another store closer to home. I could feel the emptiness inside, because it had only been five months since my son's passing. I was going through the aisles of the store, keeping it together, even with the crowded stores and the kids with their parents. Out of the blue a song came on the store's PA system, "Tears in Heaven," by Eric Clapton. He sang "Would you know my name if I saw you in heaven?" I immediately broke into tears. It took every ounce of strength to make my way back to the bathroom to have a little privacy. I sat in the stall for about twenty minutes before I could come out. My eyes at this point were as red as they could be. I ended up abandoning my cart with the items I had shopped for; I just wanted to get to my car and go home. I talked myself into going back another day.

Thanksgiving and Christmas are the two hardest holidays for me. As to Thanksgiving, my son always liked to spend it with me because he liked the dishes I made, and I would always spoil them with their favorites. Matt was a teenager and he didn't always come up to Dad's house as often as I would have liked, so if cooking his favorites is what I had to do, then I was all for it. Those are the memories that I try to remember now on those holidays. God, I miss his voice, his laughter, his smile. What I wouldn't give to wrap my arms around him again.

*

ROBERT BOOS
Robert's 21-year-old son Kevin
was killed by a drunk driver in 2015

With Kevin's death coming so close to the holiday season, it made what normally would have been the most fun time of the year an absolute nightmare. I live and work in Arizona and my family is in southern Florida, a fact that makes the holiday season even tougher. My girlfriend, Michelle, and I had thankfully decided that we were not going to go back to Florida for Thanksgiving. We went to a local steakhouse with some other friends and didn't get too caught up in the holiday. Really, I had nothing to be thankful for at all at that point, so why pretend that I did?

Christmas was another story. We decided we would go to southern Florida for a week. It was only two and half months since the death of my son, and I had absolutely no interest in holidays. None. I tried to put on a brave face for family members who were trying to enjoy it, but I just did not feel like it.

Prior to going I had an annual tradition in my office. I play Santa every year for the employee holiday party, and then on the Saturday before Christmas we host all the employees' children, a couple hundred, and let them take pictures with Santa, have cookies, all that kind of stuff. I honestly rose to the occasion. As you would imagine, I had zero interest in doing this, but when you see kids light up when they see you, like they are meeting a rock star or something, it totally transforms the moment. I humbly admit that I get into the role, and I'm very good with the kids inside that scratchy beard and giant red suit. It was actually as much fun for me as it was for them.

One of the complicating factors of traveling for Christmas is that you don't want to travel with gifts; you have to go Christmas shopping when you get home. I suddenly remembered why I did most of my shopping online and *hated* shopping malls. With this extra numb feeling and this absolute hatred of the malls at Christmas, I slogged my way through it with my girlfriend. We rarely fight, but Christmas Eve being there at the last minute was pushing both of us over the edge.

The actual holiday was okay. You brace yourself for the day and worry so badly that sometimes the big crashing wave of grief doesn't come. Oh, it hits in smaller waves, but that big crashing, stunning, take-your-breath wave didn't come. That would be later.

We split up the holiday, going to Michelle's family on Christmas Eve and to my family on Christmas day. Michelle's family was of course rather immune to what had been going on. I'm sure they were upset for me, for us, but they had moved on. Understandable. They had people from the family whom I had never met, and even some whom I had met but had not seen for a long time. I kind of just milled around and never stayed in one place too long. I got through it. There was one moment when I had to make a quick move. When they gathered for dinner they all wanted to join hands and pray or something. I excused myself and ran into the bathroom. The very last thing on Earth I wanted to be doing right then was talking to God and thanking him for everything. We weren't really on a speaking basis.

Christmas day at my family's house was a nice attempt, but highly dysfunctional. There was a very obvious and very empty chair for my son at my brother's house. Everyone was trying to be in a good mood, but it was falling very flat. I counted the minutes to get out of there. My sister-in-law's mother was in town from Puerto Rico. She is about the sweetest woman ever, and I could tell that she was missing Kevin at this event as well. Just as we were about to eat she started praying in Spanish, and I was trapped. I mean, I could make a messy exit and stumble out of the room, but I just stood there quietly, knowing she was probably thanking God for the family. I'm glad I am not fluent in Spanish.

*

RODNEY CLOUTIER
Rodney's 21-year-old fiancéee Cattie was killed by a drunk driver in 2013, and his premature daughter Dottie died in 2016

I never got to spend any holidays with either person. I can't tell you how that holidays are going to be without my daughter.

*

M.G. COY
Myrton's 56-year-old wife Maureen
died of heart failure in 2012

All holidays are very painful. At Christmas, Maureen was in the hospital and she died the day before New Year's Eve. I try to join her family on holidays; it makes them happy. But no Christmas tree. I put out a picture of Maureen, but I try to cope alone. It slowly works. I still find myself crying after four years. The pain may diminish, but it will never go away.

*

BILL DOWNS
Bill's 21-year-old son Brad and 19-year-old daughter-in-law
Samantha were killed by a drunk driver in 2007

The two main holidays as a family that we celebrated were the Fourth of July and Christmas. Though Brad enjoyed both holidays, I believe it would be safe to say that the Fourth of July was his favorite, because it was also his birthday. I always made sure the Fourth of July was very special, because not only was it his birthday, but he loved the fireworks. I'm embarrassed to say how much money we spent on fireworks, but nothing was too expensive for his birthday.

For the last eight years since the kids' death, we have overlooked the holidays due to the emotional strain it caused both Julie and I. It has been just within the past year that we have tried to have a traditional Christmas for our daughter Cindy, because we felt we were depriving her of the enjoyment of all the lights, gifts and joy this time of year brings to kids. Though she is thirty-three years of age as I write this, her mental age is that of a toddler due to her mental handicap.

The holidays are the hardest time of the year for us because of the kids not being here. We see our families celebrating, and it just sends us into an antisocial state of mind. The memories of our kids during these times is just too hard to face. We used to go all out for Christmas dinner with the kids, and now it's no different than any other dinner. It will never be easy, but we are learning to cope with the holidays one at a time.

*

JAMES FENNELL
James' 21-year-old daughter Lauren
was killed by a drunk driver in 2008

The first set of holidays were the most painful, primarily because I did not know what to expect. After going through each of them, I began to realize that the anticipation was worse than the day itself. As the years passed, I began to understand that attaching importance to the holidays is almost like people who depend upon others for their happiness. Let me explain. The day itself often brings pain, especially in the early years, but once a parent realizes that the loss is only the loss of the physical self, and that the love shared by the parent and child is eternal, the day itself tends to lose its importance.

*

MICHAEL GERSHE
Mike was 8 weeks old when his 28-year-old mom
Barbara was killed by a drunk driver in 1970
Mike was 33 when his 33-year-old best friend John
was killed in a drunk driving crash in 2004

I am Jewish, and this will probably upset my father and any rabbis reading this, but I really don't follow the traditions. I mean, I eat bacon, after all! Growing up, we did the holidays with family members and going to temple, but none of the holidays are painful because my mother wasn't alive for them. I never knew what they were like with her, so I can't say it's painful. However, I do wonder if she were alive whether I would be more observant though. I do light a menorah during Hanukkah, even though I should be the last person to light all those candles, but I think she would be proud of me for at least doing that.

In regard to Big John, the holiday season can be tough at times, because we celebrated many holidays together. His birthday is December 28, so that makes things tough too. One Christmas when he was working for Syracuse University, many of us from college gathered in Columbus, Ohio. John showed up like he was Santa Claus with bags of old Syracuse clothing. I don't think any of us go through the holidays today without thinking about that time, and many of us still have the clothes he gave us. I still have my Syracuse football sweatshirt, which is tattered and stained, but it's one of those things that is comforting around the holiday time.

I stopped celebrating Halloween after he died, because for years we had so much fun. He just brought so much life to everyone and everything that I have a hard time celebrating without him. It stinks, because I know he would want me to go out, dress up and have fun, but at the same time I think back to the times we had during Halloween and smile. Creating new memories should be something I do, but for some reason I just can't do it and still enjoy myself.

Thanksgiving is not a particularly difficult time, but I do think about the times we celebrated that holiday together. One time I was with his family, and even though we were both under age, his mom allowed me to drink wine, but not him. He protested, and I thought he was going to cry, and it was hysterically funny that his mom said no to him! Besides, watching him eat at any meal was an adventure, but Thanksgiving was a whole other event. Someone of his size could sure put away food. So now I really reflect on those times. It makes me sad that we no longer celebrate together, but I am grateful for the times we did. I am usually with my former college roommate, Bryan, and his family for Thanksgiving, so that helps. But I do miss the big guy at the table. More than anything, I miss his laughter during the holidays.

*

STEPHEN HOCHHAUS
Stephen's 51-year-old wife Kathy
died from adult soft tissue sarcoma in 2011

Christmas had always been the most special time for Kathy and me. It was also the time of my birthday, which she made so special. That first year was the hardest, for certain. We had always hosted dinner at our home for my family, and in alternate years spent it in Canada with her family. Somehow I got the courage to do it on my own and decorate the house as we always did. It took a lot of wine and many tears, but somehow I got through it. It has become easier every year since then. Setting the table with her grandma's china made it so special, but her absence was felt by all of us. Since I was the only one who could host the dinner, having this responsibility made it easier for me to pull it off. That night after everyone left was the worst part. As I looked at the tree, I descended into a very dark place.

Six years later, I find myself focusing on my grandchildren and finding more joy in their glee than in my own sorrow. Perhaps they are more of a distraction, which lessens my sorrow, but I'll take it for what it's worth. There will be times when I feel the pain, and my family understands that. I will always hang our stockings and fill them with chocolate truffles, as well as a new Swarovski crystal figurine that I would give to add to her collection. When I eat the truffles, I wonder if she enjoys them with me.

*

DAVID JONES
David's 54-year-old wife Judy
was killed by a drunk driver in 2008

For myself, the key to getting through the holidays is having lots of people around. Since my present wife, Diane, and I both lost our first spouses within two months of each other, we always feel free to talk about little things that cause us to remember them and then give each other a hug. We usually have lots of get-togethers during the holidays with little children running around, which helps a lot. Somehow being around grandchildren really helps me feel better. They demand your complete attention and keep you focused on the now instead of the past.

We always have at least one large gathering with Judy's family, and seeing her sisters helps me feel close to her. At times her sisters' voices sound very similar to Judy's which brings up memories.

I have Christmas ornaments that Judy made that always bring tears to my eyes when I hang them. They are little felt mice in walnut shell halves with long felt tails hanging down. I remember her making lots of these to pass out to the kids in our Sunday school classes. I also love to put out our four-foot-high angels made of thick plywood that I cut out using a jigsaw and Judy had painted. I put them up in the front yard with colored lights on them, and all the little kids in the neighborhood really like them.

Judy was so talented at everything she did. Whether it was creating a painting, making curtains, sewing a banner, or gardening, she wanted to do everything perfectly. I was in awe of what she could create, and during the holidays I was always looking at something she did.

Her best skill was at relationships. She was excellent at reading body language and active listening. Judy's level of empathy was off the scale, especially with children. She had a knack of being able to captivate and enchant children without even seeming to try.

On Christmas Eve we used to work a Santa Claus puzzle while waiting for the kids to fall asleep so we could put presents under the tree. At Thanksgiving she could cook fabulous meals. And in between she liked to bake cookies with the kids. Sugar cookies were the favorite, because of the creative ways they could be decorated. Today, one of my traditions is to buy a grave blanket the day after Thanksgiving and put it on her grave. Every time it snows, I use my boots to make a big heart in the snow around her grave.

On Valentine's Day I like to get out all the cards she gave me over the years and go through them. I also like to reread all the emails she sent me while I was working in England, and then look at the photos of Portsmouth when she came to visit.

I still look at myself as the luckiest man who ever lived because of the years I had Judy for my wife and lover. That was far better than fame or fortune to me, and I would not have traded a day with her for anything.

*

JOHN PETE
John's 71-year-old grandmother Tita died
from diabetes and a series of strokes in 1989

Our family is now largely spread across the country, so many of us don't see one another very often anymore. But my happiest memories will always be of spending holidays at my grandparents' home with many cousins, aunts and uncles while growing up. Holiday traditions continue to be cherished and carried on within our family, which is now spread across the country. And while there is always some sadness attached to our family losses, I try to remember lost loved ones and special times with the joy that made them so special. And that in itself is a powerful tool for coping.

*

CHAPTER EIGHT

THE EMOTIONAL RELEASE

Don't be ashamed to weep; 'tis right to grieve. Tears are only water, and flowers, trees, and fruit cannot grow without water. -BRIAN JACQUES

Crying is a natural reaction to sorrow, but many men see it as a weakness. By allowing others to witness their grief, men fear that such a display of emotion might somehow diminish their respect, power or importance. After all, men are raised to be in control, not lose it. But if grief is a deeply emotional response to loss and sometimes can't be held back, despite one's best efforts, when and where do you give in to the tears?

*

CHUCK ANDREAS
Chuck's 60-year-old wife Gloria
died unexpectedly from heart disease in 2014

I refer to crying as a meltdown, and probably the place I do it the most is in my truck, of all places. I find that the most emotional times are either first thing in the morning or at night. Driving in the morning for some reason always seems to affect me. I happen to be on the road at sunrise, and some mornings it just happens. I start thinking about Glor and hoping she is fine and that her pain is all gone. I always hope that I get to see her again and, yep, here come the tears. I will fight a meltdown if I'm around people, and even leave the room. I do not feel comfortable in front of anyone when that happens. I am fortunate enough to have keys to areas where I can be alone if I suddenly feel emotional at work. But over time I have learned to try to shut down that emotion if I can. It doesn't suddenly overwhelm me at work as much as it used to.

Nighttime is the time when I think about Glor the most, when I am in the house alone. There is just no way I can avoid it. Because of all the memories, everything I have to do now, I relate to her in the house. I'm man enough to admit that's the way I fall asleep sometimes, with tears in my eyes.

*

JEFF BALDWIN
Jeff's 20-year-old son Matthew died
in a drowning accident in 2011

There was a time when I tried to hold back my emotions. However, I found the loss too much to bear. So although for the most part I cry when I am alone, there are times when I let the tears flow anywhere. It's hard to hold them back when you have such emotions and pain inside; they have to go somewhere. I never saw my father cry but one time in his life. The door to the bathroom opened and I saw him hunched over, and my mother consoling him after the death of his sister. This was when I was ten or eleven. While it somehow instilled in me that men do not to cry, I don't conform to that rule, because there will be a song or a thought that comes to mind and cause the tears to flow.

*

ROBERT BOOS
Robert's 21-year-old son Kevin
was killed by a drunk driver in 2015

In almost fifty years of life I can count on my hand the number of times I've cried. I've teared up at a solemn event or a proud moment with my children, but it has been many years since I can remember doing actual full-out crying. It is very rare for me to cry.

I come from a family that never really expressed emotions openly and most certainly didn't cry in front of each other. Since the death of my father in 2012, I've taken on the traditional role as the family patriarch. I was the leader of the family. Leaders don't cry. Men do NOT cry. I know that's so wrong now, but that was always my thinking, and it's the thinking of most men I know.

When I got that horrible phone call on September 6, 2015, I didn't cry. The emotion was more shock and nausea than crying. I remember being on that long plane flight that morning, logged into Facebook and just looking at pictures. Tears were rolling down my face, and I turned away from the lady sitting next to me so she wouldn't see. I never really cried, though. It never came.

I can pinpoint the two times I first let go and lost it when I got home. The first time was just after landing; I was in horrible shock and hadn't slept in two days. I arrived at my brother's house where my brother, sister-in-law and mom were. I lost it a little when I first saw them, and we hugged in the living room. The real big moment was yet to come. My friend Rob and I have known each other for almost twenty years. We've coached baseball together, played poker, went to sporting events and *always* hung out with our children together. Rob's son Vincenzo was killed in the same accident as Kevin, as was Vincenzo's amazing girlfriend, Morgan.

Of all the people in my family and all my friends, Rob was the one person I wanted to see. Not only were we the best of friends for a long time, but he *knew*. He was going through exactly what I was going through at the exact same time. That's why the only comfort I was going to gain anytime soon was being in the same room as him and talking to him.

When I got to his house there was a crowd of people there. I found my way through the crowd and acknowledged and hugged twenty or more people trying to find Rob. There were a lot of people there. Of course I talked to all of them and accepted their condolences. I hugged more people in those five minutes than I probably have in my whole life. I'm not a hugger. I just don't do that, but in this moment and in the next few weeks, it would seem to be the natural thing to do.

So I finally saw Rob across the room and made my way over to him. Have we ever hugged in our entire lives? Probably a couple of times in those manly-type moments — more like a power hug. This was anything but. This was two fathers, each of whom was one day into losing his most precious asset — his son. We both fell apart and just hung on to each other; I'm not sure if it was ten seconds or ten minutes. I'm pretty sure fifty people were watching us, and I'm pretty sure it was quite a sight, but I don't care. For once I was the person at this center of attention and I was doing exactly what I should have been doing. I was mourning my loss with someone who knew *exactly* how I felt, and felt exactly the same way.

I did not cry at my son's wake or funeral, or at the services of the other two kids. It just never came. I was deeply sad and so much in shock that I was never even close to losing it. When we were at the service for my son in front of about eight hundred people, that was the time you would think I would be most at risk to lose it and bawl, but I held it together. Even listening to my friends, Kevin's mom and my other children talk about their brother was unbelievably sad, but it didn't push me over the edge. When it came my turn as the final speaker, I told funny stories about Kevin and how much he loved people. I never lost it once.

In the week after my son's funeral I had a couple of moments of crying when I was alone. Mostly at the end of those long days and in the shower by myself, I'd think about my son and would lose it. It's very safe to lose it where nobody can hear or see, and that's the only time I would feel comfortable about it.

Now, much later in the process, I can see how I have been impacted by all this, and I am much more vulnerable to any type of emotional issues. Just about a month after Kevin's death, the movie "The Martian" came out in theaters. I had read the book from cover to cover in the previous year, and *loved* it. One of the very last things I felt like doing in the weeks after losing my son was to go and enjoy a movie, yet this movie called to me. I really wanted to see it. When you are in the first part of grief, the very numb and bewildered phase, any type of normal enjoyment seems very foreign to you. It's almost like you are at a party that you weren't invited to, and you try to sink into a chair and disappear. That's how I felt in the movie theater. I had several impulses to stand up and say, "I don't belong here..." and run out. But I didn't.

The movie was great. It held up to the book, and was a very powerful story about human survival and spirit. If you haven't seen it, I don't want to give away the ending, but let's just say it has a rather positive ending. When this was shown on the screen, I was happy for the character yet I immediately thought of my son lying in his grave. I was devastated and left the theater with tears streaming down my face, hoping that nobody would notice.

That sensitivity to emotion only grew stronger as the days grew into months. Any emotions involving parents and children made me a wreck. Take the Little League World Series, for example. Great emotional stories were shown about twelve-year-old kids playing baseball and how proud and excited their parents were. It tore me up. Going the other way with that, when the young child was killed by the alligator at Walt Disney World, I immediately put myself in the place of the parents and the absolute horror they went through, and I was an absolute wreck for days. Of course, nobody knows this. I don't think anyone has ever caught me crying. I plan to keep it this way.

*

RODNEY CLOUTIER
Rodney's 21-year-old fiancéee Cattie was killed by a drunk
driver in 2013, and his premature daughter Dottie died in 2016

I have cried while driving, at home in the living room, and in the garage.

*

BILL DOWNS
Bill's 21-year-old son Brad and 19-year-old daughter-in-law
Samantha were killed by a drunk driver in 2007

At the time of the kids' death, I would cry at the drop of a hat. Then as I began getting back into the work routine I would tear up when my fellow employees would ask how I was doing. I would have to excuse myself and go to the restroom to hide my tears. When I drove my work van, and even driving home, tears would flow uncontrollably. I always tried to hide my emotions from my wife, Julie, and everyone else for that matter. I was always taught that men were not supposed to cry. I would always hold it in as long as I could, and when it did come out I would weep uncontrollably. Today, nine years later, I find that if I have to let some tears flow, I do. I have earned the right to show emotion; and Julie and I have no reason to hide our emotions.

*

JAMES FENNELL
James' 21-year-old daughter Lauren
was killed by a drunk driver in 2008

I believe the car provides a degree of safety for most men. When driving alone, one is insulated from the outside world and from interaction with others. In our society, a man who cries is often not looked upon favorably, at least not by other men. I can remember having to clean my glasses every couple of minutes while driving because of the tears that would flow. However, I always felt that the tears were a necessary part of the grieving process, and to hold them back would merely be going around the grief process when I actually need to be going through the process in order to heal.

*

MICHAEL GERSHE
Mike was 8 weeks old when his 28-year-old mom
Barbara was killed by a drunk driver in 1970
Mike was 33 when his 33-year-old best friend John
was killed in a drunk driving crash in 2004

Wow, where do I cry? I cry on my couch while watching the end of "Field of Dreams." I cry when there is a television show and a mother dies, or an extremely sensitive moment between a mother and child. I cry because I wish I had just one moment like that. In the last season of "The Flash," when the character went back in time to save his mother, I was in tears because I wished I had the power to do the very same.

I've cried on stage when presenting my program as I am talking about my mother. I don't cry all the time, but I get so emotional at times that I break down. If you think it's hard crying in front of one person, try doing it in front of two hundred or more! But most of the time I cry when I am alone because, let's face it, I'm a guy. We don't want to seem weak. But the older I get, the more I think that crying in front of others is a sign of strength — maybe.

In regard to Big John, I probably cry the most when alone in the car. When I visit him at the cemetery, I have sat in the car before walking to his grave and listened to the Billy Joel song "Piano Man," which was one of his favorite songs. That does bring on the waterworks. There may be times when I am driving and have some random thought of him and I will get choked up thinking of him. I've been on my couch and cried, but I am also alone at those times.

In terms of crying in front of someone, heck, I've done it on stage in front of strangers when I share his story, but within my circle of friends I have plenty of people I would feel comfortable crying in front of when it comes to John. My friends who knew John make me feel safer, because we all loved him like a brother and understand the pain of his loss. Perhaps it's a case of misery loves company, but I could cry in front of my friends Sean, Brent, Dennis, Bryan, Andy, Matt, and Melissa and would hope they feel the same.

*

STEPHEN HOCHHAUS
Stephen's 51-year-old wife Kathy
died from adult soft tissue sarcoma in 2011

I find that I cry only when I am alone now. This wasn't the case in my first year, however, and I would find myself losing it with close family members. During the first several months of my grief's journey I realized I was crying in my sleep. At first I thought I must have had an eye infection, for I would wake up with my face stuck to my pillow. I understood quickly what was going on, and it happened less as time went by. At work I had many distractions that kept the tears at bay, yet I would sometimes hit a trigger and run to the bathroom to compose myself. This mostly occurred when I would see Kathy's handwriting in the bookkeeping which was her end of the business. When I would get home, however, it got a lot worse. As soon as I would open the garage door and see her car inside, bam, there was the first trigger. She had always been there to greet me, and I understood at those moments that that was never to be again.

Inside me I had triggers of all descriptions. How could it be any other way, for we lived together? We really lived together as if we were one. The crying lessened as time went by. Yet watching a favorite movie or television program of hers would, and still can, cause the tears to flow. The biggest trigger for me, however, was music. Certain songs would set me off, and that would occur in my car as well. Shortly after Kathy was gone I found her iPod in the office desk drawer at home. This iPod was one she used when taking her morning walks, and I started listening to it. It contained music which included songs we both loved and also songs I had never heard before. It also had two songs which spoke to life after death, which hit me like a ton of bricks. It was almost as if she had known something and left it for me to find.

Several months after her death I had to drive from Arizona to Alberta to close our condo down and bring some personal items back. I took her iPod with me and listened to her music all the way up. I cried a lot in the car on that trip, I can tell you. I have since added new songs to her playlist that speak to me about the love we had for each other. Now, six years later, I can say I cry a lot less. Perhaps a few times a week it will happen, but every so often on a weekend it hits me quite hard. I have come to think of triggers as landmines carefully laid by two loving people, to be struck by the surviving spouse. When I hit one of those landmines, I feel better knowing that I would not hurt so much had I not loved her so deeply.

*

DAVID JONES
David's 54-year-old wife Judy
was killed by a drunk driver in 2008

In the beginning I cried mostly at home in the evenings. Then it was most often when I visited her grave. Now it is usually when I see something with her handwriting or that she made. I Also cry when key dates and holidays happen. As I write, in two days it will be eight years since Judy's death. That day and our anniversary are the two hardest days for me.

*

JOHN PETE
John's 71-year-old grandmother Tita died
from diabetes and a series of strokes in 1989

I am comfortable sharing heartfelt tears with close family members and friends when we have lost mutual loved ones and beloved pets. But crying alone is also important, because there are no inhibitions that may cause you to restrain yourself.

I think it can be harder for men to openly express emotions because many men take on roles of showing strength, protectiveness and comforting others in crisis in our society. And certainly some men are raised with a belief that showing outward emotions is a sign of weakness.

*

ROBERT RIECK
Robert's 18-year-old daughter
Ashley died by suicide in 2016

I try to hide it from my other kids. Usually I go to the lake where she died to cry, or when driving, or when home alone. I guess I don't count how often, but it's at least three or four times a week. Early in the morning or really late at night.

*

We do not remember days.
We remember moments.

CESARE PAVESE

*

CHAPTER NINE

THE DARKNESS

Walking with a friend in the dark is better than
walking alone in the light. -HELEN KELLER

Grief pushed to the far corners of our thoughts can lead to darker
thoughts. Rage, self-harm and suicidal thoughts occur for some in
the immediate aftermath of profound loss, yet few readily admit it
for fear of being judged or condemned. While there would be no
rainbow without the rain, where do we find the energy to weather
the dark storm?

*

CHUCK ANDREAS
Chuck's 60-year-old wife Gloria
died unexpectedly from heart disease in 2014

When I started this, I promised myself that I would be open
and honest. I need to explain some background first. My mom was
diagnosed with terminal cancer a few years ago. We received the
call one night at 2 a.m. that she had passed, and would we come to
her apartment? To this day, I don't know why I didn't think this
through. When Glor and I went into her apartment, there was my
mom, passed away on a hospital bed. I don't know why I didn't
realize that was the way it would be, but I didn't.

During my mom's funeral home setting, I don't recall seeing her in the casket. All I remember is seeing her when I entered the apartment. I talked to Glor about it and said, "Please, I never want to be put in that situation again." Unfortunately, that's how I found Glor, passed away in our bed. I cannot get that out of my head. The person I loved more than anything passed away. This sticks with me to this day.

One night when I was drinking by myself at home, I opened a bottle of liquor to go along with my beer. After finishing the bottle I went in and sat on the bed and thought about how I would never get that sight out of my head, and tried to think how could I? I came to the decision that the only way to get it out of my head was to commit suicide. I grabbed the gun and the bullets, and then loaded the gun. I decided I didn't have to write a note, because I would be found on the bed where my wife died and it would be self-explanatory. I thought all my kids are big enough, they all have kids, and they don't need me anymore. Then I thought of who would find me. The one person who checks on me is my stepdaughter Alecia, and if I didn't respond she has a key. So Alecia and Heather would be the ones to find me. I realize that drunks aren't smart, but I was thinking, Chuck, you can't handle finding Glor passed away, and here you are going to run from your problem and pass it on to the two girls.

Needless to say, I don't really drink anymore. Alecia asked me to get the gun out of the house, and I did. I will just deal with this the best I can.

*

JEFF BALDWIN
Jeff's 20-year-old son Matthew died
in a drowning accident in 2011

When I got the news that my son had drowned, all I wanted to do was to be with him. I prayed to God to just let me go and be with Matthew. I prayed that God would just once maybe give me a free pass to heaven. I contemplated suicide two times. However, I know that it goes against my religion and beliefs to take such actions into my own hands, and that somewhere in the mix of things I had a cause or purpose remaining for me here. But in the back of my mind I can relate to people who check out by suicide, because once you had the thought yourself, it's easy to relate to

*

ROBERT BOOS
Robert's 21-year-old son Kevin
was killed by a drunk driver in 2015

I think it's important to be very clear with a question like this. At no time and for not one moment did I ever consider or think about harming myself. What was stunning, and what did happen, is that I immediately lost any fear of my eventual death. It could come tomorrow or it could come thirty years from now. I welcome its arrival, when before Kevin's death I would never have even thought of it. I would probably have fought tooth and nail, with everything I had prior to my son's death. Now, it's what it is. If it's my time, come get me. I won't run.

Another very tangible and very strong thought I had from the moment I saw Kevin lying in a casket at the funeral home was this that I would trade places with him in a moment. With zero hesitation and instantly, if I could push a button and trade places with him, I would. I would do it with a smile on my face and without any doubt in my mind. Unfortunately, I don't think God or whoever is in charge of matters like this will negotiate this fact. But I know I would. One thousand percent.

I wrote earlier about my one moment of rage two days after my son's death. As I was driving to the funeral home to make arrangements, some careless jerk cut me off with his car. This was absolute rage, something I have never felt before and have never seen. I actually saw the color red. It took the urgent voice of my daughter to bring me back from the abyss. Had I gotten to that guy in this state, I'm not sure what might have happened.

Someday very soon I will have another deep and dark set of emotions that I will need to confront head-on. We have the time when we will face the murdering drunk driver who killed our three beautiful children. I know as a man that this time for me, for my friend Rob, Vincenzo's dad, and for Ken, Morgan's dad, will be especially difficult. Our primal instincts are at play here, and some of those instincts are not appropriate for a courtroom setting. Let's just leave it at that.

*

RODNEY CLOUTIER
Rodney's 21-year-old fiancée Cattie was killed by a drunk
driver in 2013, and his premature daughter Dottie died in 2016

I never contemplated self harm. I had others to look after.

*

BILL DOWNS
Bill's 21-year-old son Brad and 19-year-old daughter-in-law
Samantha were killed by a drunk driver in 2007

I began cutting myself to have an outlet for the pain and guilt. I truly believed I was at fault for the kids' death because I did not protect them from the impaired driver. My guilt turned to rage and hate. I could not understand how a God of mercy and grace could let three innocent kids' lives be snuffed out in an instant. I turned my hurt and grief against God, and it began to drive me insane. I even took my anger out on my wife, Julie. I was so out of my head with anger and rage. It finally came to a head; I was losing my grip on life and my family, so I decided to end my life. I was finished with resisting the grip my grief had on my mind. The only way I saw out of it was to take my life. I couldn't face my wife or my daughter because I was so ashamed of myself, and I no longer believed in a merciful God. Death was the only answer I could see.

Julie never gave up on me, even after throwing me out. She had seen all she could take, and told me to leave. That was the night I tried to take my life. But God had other plans for us, and for me. He saved my life, and Julie's prayers were answered. God not only saved my life, but he saved my soul. I am no longer angry with God, with Julie, with the world. His saving grace gave me a chance to change a negative into a positive. Each day that goes by, I live my life for God, for Julie, and our daughter Cindy, and to be a voice for my three kids who were stolen from us.

*

JAMES FENNELL
James' 21-year-old daughter Lauren
was killed by a drunk driver in 2008

Thankfully, I have never experienced any dark thoughts or harmful actions. I always felt that I owed it to my daughter and to my remaining family to try to be the best person I could be for them, and especially in respect to my daughter's memory. As a result, I was never tempted to drift in that direction.

*

JEFF GARDNER
Jeff's 18-year-old daughter Cassidy
was killed by a drugged driver in 2013

I have not had suicidal thoughts. I felt guilty for not being able to protect Cassidy. My mother committed suicide when she was forty-one years old. I was twenty at the time. I would never want to miss out on my kids' life and the time I have with my wife.

*

MICHAEL GERSHE
Mike was 8 weeks old when his 28-year-old mom
Barbara was killed by a drunk driver in 1970
Mike was 33 when his 33-year-old best friend John
was killed in a drunk driving crash in 2004

I use humor to hide my darker thoughts all the time. Being a comedian, I use humor as a defense mechanism and to avoid anything serious. I have experienced more anger than full-on rage and thoughts of suicide during my forty-six years.

In my early twenties, life wasn't going so well for me. I was in a lot of mental pain because I thought a lot about my mother. I wanted to know if she was safe and at peace. I was, and always will be, a boy who wants his mother. I lived on the fifteenth floor of my apartment complex and was ready to jump out the next morning. I just wanted to feel her comfort and to stop feeling this pain that I couldn't stop for some reason. I went to sleep and dreamed that I met her. She said she was safe and I shouldn't worry about her, and she gave me a hug. I woke up suddenly, face down in the pillow with my arms crossed as if I were hugging her. Since then, whenever I have those feelings I think of that dream. I know she didn't sacrifice her life to save me so I could do something stupid to end my life early.

Whatever anger I have toward the drunk driver, or God, or drunk drivers whom I read about who injure or kill others, I was kept alive for a purpose. While I may never stop grieving my mother, I won't do anything stupid to embarrass her by ending my life either.

In the twelve years since John's been gone, I've had quite a few darker thoughts that might have had some suicidal tendencies. The same with my thoughts about my mother being gone; it's a feeling of emptiness and pain that sometimes is so strong that I just want it to end. But the one thing I have learned about John's death is the impact it had on his family and friends. I realized that if I did something stupid, well, I just couldn't put my family and friends through the same thing. Besides, if there is an afterlife where we meet our loved ones, Big John would kick my ass. So when I do have those thoughts, I remember the phone calls, his wake, his funeral, and the visits to his gravesite, and that helps erase those darker thoughts.

*

STEPHEN HOCHHAUS
Stephen's 51-year-old wife Kathy
died from adult soft tissue sarcoma in 2011

From the first week of losing Kathy, I had very strong thoughts of wishing I could die. The desire for death was more about being able to go after her before she could get too far away. An awful lot of strange thoughts can go through a guy's mind, for we don't think so clearly at first. I doubt I could have killed myself, for when I thought of my own death I also thought about what that would be like for my sons and grandchildren. I just couldn't be that selfish. When I was flying with my wife's ashes up to Canada I wished the plane would crash, but then thought about how unfair that would be to the others on the plane. So I let that one go. In time, I went from wishing I were dead to being okay with dying; to being ready to go, while wanting to live as best as I could. Today I want to enjoy what time I have left and experience all I can, as Kathy and I would have done together.

*

DAVID JONES
David's 54-year-old wife Judy
was killed by a drunk driver in 2008

I have experienced a few moments of anger, but never considered self-harm or suicide. I have always been quite stable and optimistic. I also consider it important to be there for my children and grandchildren.

*

JOHN PETE
John's 71-year-old grandmother Tita died
from diabetes and a series of strokes in 1989

Because I have worked in the field of grief, I am familiar with anger and self-destructive thoughts, and understand the importance of support. I sometimes long to be with my loved ones who have died, but never to the point of seriously considering self-harm. Grief-related anger, on the other hand, is something I have experienced firsthand. After one particularly difficult loss, I found myself losing my temper with innocent bystanders, such as store clerks, over pretty mundane things. From that I learned how important it is to have appropriate ways to vent grief every single day so it doesn't erupt in bursts of pain and anger.

*

ROBERT RIECK
Robert's 18-year-old daughter
Ashley died by suicide in 2016

I have often thought about joining her, but that seems to be an easy way out from this grief I feel. I have four daughters who need me, so I always hope that I can get past those many late-night feelings of loss and failure. I sometimes get very angry at certain people who were in Ashley's life and were aware of her thoughts leading up to that dreadful morning.

*

There is a land of the living and a land
of the dead, and the bridge is love.

THORNTON WILDER

*

CHAPTER TEN

THE PHYSICAL EXPRESSIONS

I would rather be physically hurt than emotionally.
Because you can put a bandage on your finger,
but you can't put one on your heart. -ANONYMOUS

Emotions are the body's energetic release valve, but uncomfortable with an open display of emotion, men commonly use physical expression as an outlet for grief. Some work longer hours, turn to heavy manual labor like chopping wood, or resort to physical abuse. What forms of physical expression have you used as an outlet for your sorrow?

*

JEFF BALDWIN
Jeff's 20-year-old son Matthew died
in a drowning accident in 2011

I went into a deep depression. In a period of just five months, I lost my mother and my precious son. People stopped calling to check on me, and everyone just scattered back to their own lives. I have been on a downward spiral for about five years now. I have let myself go and my health is not good. I am fifty-one years old and I feel sixty-plus inside. I abused my prescribed pain medication to somehow numb the pain, which led me down a darker path. I gained over a hundred pounds and now I am plagued with health issues. As much as I try to heal and get myself back on track, I just don't have the fight in me anymore. But I am still fighting the fight; I just need to find what my purpose is in life now that I have to walk this road on my own. It's hard and lonely, but I know deep down that it's a road that I must walk along because somewhere on this road, I will learn a lot of helpful knowledge about loss that is meant to be shared with others who are just starting this journey. In the end, life is all about helping others so onward I go.

*

ROBERT BOOS
Robert's 21-year-old son Kevin
was killed by a drunk driver in 2015

The absolute worst times for this grief journey are quiet times when I am doing nothing. I have learned to avoid quiet times at all costs. I always have something going on or something to do. It has brought me close to total exhaustion more than once, but it keeps my mind occupied. Thankfully, I have a job that requires seventy hours or more per week to keep it going. I am responsible for two hundred and twenty-five people in a large office environment. Days are jam-packed with things to do, and this keeps my mind busy instead of suffering, thinking about Kevin.

While I say that work has been a blessing, it was not like that when I first came back. Kevin was killed on Labor Day weekend in 2015, September 6, to be exact. I returned to work two weeks and one day later, on September 21, 2015. I would like to tell you a detailed story of how I did on that day and how I got through it, but I really don't remember. I remember driving to the building and going inside. I'm pretty sure the other managers in the building put out a request to the staff to give me some breathing space, because although everyone was friendly and glad I was back, there was a very respectable distance kept. When I go back and think about it, I would say it is one of the true acts of kindness I experienced in this whole ordeal, the thought to let me ease my way back in, at my speed and during my timeline. I could not have asked for a more supportive group.

Of course, my personality didn't allow that to happen for very long. I was quiet for about a day and then tried to immerse myself back into the flow of a huge office with hundreds of people. It was good to be busy.

It also brought feelings of guilt that I didn't expect. How dare I go on with my life and try to get back to work! My son was killed. I should be lying in bed and not moving at all. Trust me, a big part of me wanted to do this.

What was disturbing during this transition back to work was the flashbacks or the "movie reel" that I had read about. If I was in a meeting and leading the discussion, then all was well. If I was very involved in a conversation, then we went along fairly well. It was those moments when someone else was talking that the movie reel would start playing. I was reliving the accident (that I hadn't seen) in my head. What did my son see? Did he know what happened? Did he live long or was he gone instantly? What did his friends see? Did they know they had been hit by a drunk going 100 mph on a city street? Both of Kevin's friends died at the hospital, but Kevin never made it out of the vehicle. All of that was going through my head while conversations were being held in front of me, yet I was lost deep in those thoughts.

Why did they stop the effort to get my son out of the car? Was he that dead that they stop trying? When they gave up on him and worked on getting the two friends out of the backseat, what did they do with Kevin? He was there in the car. I hope they covered him up or something. I guess they would, right? "So, Bob do you like that plan?" And suddenly I'm back to reality.

"What plan?" I apologized, and asked the person to repeat what he or she just said. I was reliving my son's death. Again. That was the movie reel. A horrible film that keeps playing. Different scenes and some repeats. But over and over again. For months.

What were also very disturbing were flashbacks. I would be sitting in some of the same meetings or actually even talking to a person, and behind his back I would see my son's casket and him lying in it. I could see his sleeping face and also the orange blush they put on his face to mask the signs of death. I would look away and look at someone else, only to turn back to the original person, and there sat the casket. This lasted for months before it finally started to fade.

*

RODNEY CLOUTIER
Rodney's 21-year-old fiancéee Cattie was killed by a drunk
driver in 2013, and his premature daughter Dottie died in 2016

I have no clue as to what has changed. I do know it's brought me close to my current family and is causing me to fight twice as hard for custody of one of my kids. So, in a sense I'm taking the anger and hatred and flipping it for the good side.

*

BILL DOWNS
Bill's 21-year-old son Brad and 19-year-old daughter-in-law
Samantha were killed by a drunk driver in 2007

After Julie and I went through grief and marriage counseling, I found the easiest way to deal with my grief was to just sit down and talk to Julie and share our grief with each other. I spend time in prayer and Bible study. Julie and I accept our grief by turning that grief into compassion for the members of the support groups we created for victims on Facebook. We have turned our grief into talking to others about losing someone because of an impaired driver. We put our grief into words and have co-authored one book and are working on others. By doing this, we believe we can help others who have lost loved ones.

*

JAMES FENNELL
James' 21-year-old daughter Lauren
was killed by a drunk driver in 2008

I needed something to attempt to help myself provide relief from the continuing pain in the early days. Fortunately, I had my own business and could turn my efforts toward my work rather easily. My mind, if idle for too long a period of time, would begin to take me down the path of what might have ended in depression. For my mental and physical health, it was most helpful for me to turn my efforts toward my work. As the months passed, I began to scale back the number of hours and only worked long days when the demands of the business required it. In time, the need to keep my mind busy was replaced by a need to reach out to try to help newly bereaved parents. Of course, by helping them I was also helping myself.

*

MICHAEL GERSHE
Mike was 8 weeks old when his 28-year-old mom
Barbara was killed by a drunk driver in 1970
Mike was 33 when his 33-year-old best friend John
was killed in a drunk driving crash in 2004

In college, swimming was my physical outlet for grief because

I had my alone time and I could take out whatever anger I had in the water. I never punched walls or abused myself physically or with alcohol. I always used a healthy way to grieve physically. I don't swim now, but I still workout or ride my bike or hike where I can just turn inward with my own thoughts to think about life. Here in northeast Ohio, I love our park systems and enjoy the peace of nature. It makes me appreciate the fact that I am alive. Then again, food is another awesome outlet that I've indulged in at times. There is nothing that a Dairy Queen Blizzard can't make better!

*

STEPHEN HOCHHAUS
Stephen's 51-year-old wife Kathy
died from adult soft tissue sarcoma in 2011

I wish I had used physical labor to express my grief, but instead I chose eating. I used comfort food as a relief from pain. I did work longer hours, but that was to recover from all the medical bills left behind and work myself out of debt. I expressed my grief mostly by writing. I joined a grief support group online and wrote daily. I contributed to a blog and read many others' writings. It was more than just a release and expression of my grief. It became a way of paying back the help I received when I needed it most. Lately I have become a fundraiser to help keep a website going which helps so many grieving souls. This has become a way to channel my grief into something productive and gives me a good feeling even when I am sad. For me, this is really a big deal. I have come to realize that grief is always changing. Time has a way of doing that. So as I look to the future, I wonder where I will be tomorrow.

*

DAVID JONES
David's 54-year-old wife Judy
was killed by a drunk driver in 2008

Initially I worked out in the gym for an hour or two every night. It helped me to cope, and even after eight years I try to work out every day for at least forty-five minutes.

*

JOHN PETE
John's 71-year-old grandmother Tita died
from diabetes and a series of strokes in 1989

I have used many different things on different days to help me cope with grief, such as taking long walk with my dogs, writing, and art, all of which I find to be good brief distractions from difficult grief.

I learned that early on in the grief process you just need to feel your grief and absorb the reality of your loss. Along the way it also becomes helpful to engage in things that nurture you, to help you accept and adjust to the permanent absence of your loved one.

Writing and art are things I do consistently whether I am grieving or not, but they are especially helpful as a tool for coping with grief. Through personal losses I have learned that doing nothing is just not an option for me.

I often say to others that it's okay to grieve and it's okay to embrace healing, too. Grief is a natural process, but I have learned that you can help yourself in so many ways, as a part of that. Men and women commonly express grief differently, but I believe it's important to focus more on each person's individual experiences as a basis for needed support.

*

ROBERT RIECK
Robert's 18-year-old daughter
Ashley died by suicide in 2016

My physical expression usually is in the form of working a lot to get my mind off of the feelings. I also do things with the other girls that I may not have done as often as I should have. I also decided to end my marriage of twenty-two years, as I was so tired of being so unhappy. When my daughter committed suicide, it really put some things in my life into perspective. I knew that if I did not make some changes, I was definitely headed to suicide. I also joined a gym but that only lasted a couple of months. Unfortunately, I started smoking a lot more and drinking to sleep at night.

*

CHAPTER ELEVEN

THE RELATIONSHIPS

How people treat you is their karma; how you react
is yours. - WAYNE DYER

Because everyone processes loss in his or her own way, the journey
through the aftermath can strain even the closest relationships.
Some bonds remain steady, dependable and faithful while others
fall away. What relationships were impacted the most following the
loss of your loved one?

*

CHUCK ANDREAS
Chuck's 60-year-old wife Gloria
died unexpectedly from heart disease in 2014

From my loss of Glor, my family and hers have done a nice job
of trying to keep me involved in family get-togethers. I actually
have more contact now with my sister Kim. She makes sure I am
doing all right, as does my stepdaughter Alecia and my daughter
Ashley. I lost my best friend before Glor passed away, so the two
people I would talk to the most are now gone. I guess I should feel
lucky, because I have some people who check in on me. Ron calls
once a week to see if I need anything and Dennis checks in and

stops over. I have a married couple who I've been friends with for years, Hedgey and Patty. They always invite me to their house, or just call to say hi. I have noticed several things, though. The number of friends who said "Hey, I'll give you a call," yet never do. The other is "Hey, we'll have you over," and never do.

I have a close friend who lost his wife before Glor passed away, and we would talk once a week. Then after Glor passed away, he found a girlfriend. Do you think I hear from him now? No, he rarely answers his phone. The thing that bothers me the most is that when he needed me and had thoughts of suicide, I was there for him.

I've noticed that when I'm out shopping or just out of the house when I'm approached by someone I know, it seems that he or she is tentative and the questions seem guarded or careful. It would be nice to have someone come up like it used to be, just easy and relaxed. I understand that I have a reputation of not being the easiest person to approach, but that's just what people assume; it's not the way it really is. I guess when it comes down to it, besides the people I've mentioned, the phone has stopped ringing.

When it comes to strained or disconnected relationships, my late mom, Glor and family always said I need to forgive. But I don't.

*

JEFF BALDWIN
Jeff's 20-year-old son Matthew died
in a drowning accident in 2011

I have lost a handful of what I thought were close friends I could count on. However, in the weeks and months following my son's passing, it was almost like a taboo of sorts to bring up my son's name. My friends would avoid the subject at great length. Then one day someone I thought so much of and was in my close circle of friends came out and said, "Shouldn't you be healing and past the grief?" Honestly, those were the words that came out of his mouth. I excused myself to get away from the situation. I couldn't contain myself and was just blown away that he would say such hurtful words. Those so-called friends drifted away, but I don't hold any bad feelings inside, because deep down in my heart I personally feel that people are genuine and truly don't know what to say in a situation when someone has lost a child. They do their best, but those words can hurt the person who is in deep grief over his or her loss. I wish there were a book to help educate people on how to deal with friends who have lost a child.

*

ROBERT BOOS
Robert's 21-year-old son Kevin
was killed by a drunk driver in 2015

One thing grief will do is quickly thin out the herd. You soon learn that your very true and dear friends never leave you; that they come even closer during a time of horrible loss. You also learn that those who are really just people you know, and not truly friends, might make an appearance at the spectacle of the funeral or memorial service, yet quickly fade into the background. I think I should be offended at all of that, but I'm really not. It saves me the burden of having to fake niceties and friendship with them.

There were a couple of friends, most notably my brother-in-law and childhood best friend, Andy. Andy was my voice when I didn't have a voice. During that initial shock and numbness of the week after, Andy stood next to me and got me through funeral arrangements and burial plans. He is an elder at his church, so he also led the memorial service and graveside prayers. After I got back to Arizona I sent him a handwritten letter telling him how much he meant to me, and how much that time meant to me. It was probably the most vulnerable note I've ever written, and yet it felt good to write it all out. We were such Star Trek freaks our whole lives that once we even played Kirk and Spock in a video (stop laughing, please). So I'm hoping my saying "I have been and forever shall be your friend" hit home in that card.

Another friend of mine, Israel, is a pastor in his church. We have worked as high school football officials many years together, and I always found him to be such an absolute joy to be around. When Kevin was killed, I received hundreds of text messages of condolence. It is nearly impossible to respond to any of them, but I was drawn to Israel's. I know him mostly from football, but also know him to be a very spiritual man and a good friend. I asked him to speak at Kevin's memorial service. Kevin would not want a priest or a formal religious service, but I know he would have been pleased that his Uncle Andy and my friend Israel were there for it.

You also can gain friends or grow an existing friendship during a time of grief. I would bet that it is very rare to do this, but I believe I have in a couple of cases.

My friends Rob and Roxana lost their son Vincenzo in the same drunk driving crash in which we lost Kevin. Kevin and Vincenzo had been friends since they played Little League baseball together when they were just very young boys. This group also included our friends John, Bridget, Susan, and Shelly. We lovingly called ourselves the "A-List." We were all leaders on the baseball league and worked side by side for ten years. We went on vacations together with the kids, all twenty of us. We went out to dinner together, and celebrated birthdays and holidays together. To think that two of our families would lose our children in this terrible crash is unfathomable.

The part about Rob and Roxana that I want to mention is hard to explain. The fact that they lost their son at the same time is unimaginable. It's also a pain that is impossible to describe; you have to have lost something this precious to be able to comprehend it. The tough thing to explain is this: I would give anything for them not to have lost Vincenzo. I wish they didn't know exactly what this is like and the day-to-day pain that this causes. Yet I'm so thankful that they are here for me and that I'm here for them, despite the horrible circumstances. I'm not sure what I would have done without them. The only time of any peace during the week of that triple loss was when I was at their house sitting around their table and talking about what happened. There is a certain "in the know" feeling that you have and that only others who have lost this much understand.

I did gain some very good friends in this tragedy. Ken and Lisa, as well as their daughter Hayley, are the family of Morgan. Morgan was lost in the accident with the boys, and we were quickly thrown together as parents who have lost these three. I quickly gained a kinship to Ken and Lisa, as we were all sharing this same horrible time. Some of the few times of comfort I have had since these deaths are the moments I can sit and talk with Ken and Lisa in person. We have truly been able to share some of the most intimate details of the loss, ask questions of each other about how we handled certain moments, and rely on each other for comfort. Most times there really is not any comfort, but just the ability to talk to someone who *knows* is a big help.

Hayley has been a great help to my daughter Shannon. They have both lost precious siblings whom both were very close to, and I know they talk a lot. I do not believe anyone who has not lost a child understands the depth of this pain and despair, and I certainly recognize that I do not fully comprehend the feelings that Shannon and Hayley go through every day. I'm glad they are there for one another.

Family is another story. My relationship with my two surviving children is a lot stronger and closer than it was prior to Kevin's death. Not that it wasn't great before that—I always thought it was. Even with me living on the other side of the country, I was always very involved with my children's lives and communicated constantly via phone or text messaging.

When you lose a child, a natural instinct is to become over protective of your surviving children. This is most certainly true. Although I tried not to let them notice it, I was more inquisitive and more curious about their daily tasks, whereabouts and plans. My daughter calls it stalking. I prefer "over parenting of a grown adult child." No matter, I have no regrets about that—it was survival to me, to be there daily for them, although I didn't sleep for months.

I feel like my son and my daughter are closer now than we have ever been, maybe even more so. Kevin would be so proud. He loved his brother and his sister very much, and when there were rough patches between them it always bothered Kevin. Just before his death, the three of them had a very long FaceTime conversation where they cleared the air about any difficulties. I remember Kevin telling me how happy he was that they all had the chance to talk.

My girlfriend, Michelle, has been amazing. She was by my side during the week of the funeral and the memorial services and took care of me those days. I really do not know how I functioned.

The only bump we had is that she had lost her husband to an illness a few years ago and obviously went through something similar. She was able to move on with her life and tried to make the same correlation with the loss of my son. But it didn't go over well.

Thankfully, those comments stopped and she realized that this was a much different type of ordeal. I had told her the week of the funeral that if she took her stuff and went running I wouldn't blame her, because I knew what I know right now: I will never be the same person again. I'm pleased to report almost a year later that she is still by my side and still very supportive. We attended The Compassionate Friends national conference in Phoenix, Arizona, a few months ago. She was very attentive and interested in all the talks and therapy-type sessions. I think she also got a very good idea of what it is all about from other people who have lost what we have lost

I know my mother has had a particularly difficult time with Kevin's death. She would never admit it, but I'm sure he was her favorite. Not for any particular reason, but just because he was always the quiet and shy one. Mom lost my brother Jeffrey in infancy, so she has been through the loss of a child, even though it was over forty-five years ago. My oldest son, Jeffrey, is named in my late brother's honor. I am sorry that in her loss and her sadness over his death I am unable to talk to her about it without her getting upset. There is time in a man's life when he needs to talk to his mom, and I haven't really been able to.

Kevin's middle name was Kyle, my younger brother's name. Kevin and his Uncle Kyle were very close as well, and I know it's very hard for Kyle to talk about. Kyle's wife, Lily, and Kevin were exceptionally close; in fact, they had just gone out together to celebrate Kevin's twenty-first birthday a few months before his death. So that is our family dynamic: very hurt by loss, and yet we really don't speak of it.

I'm honestly very tired, most of the time physically exhausted, because my job is that demanding and I'm always doing something, but I'm talking about being mentally tired. The withdrawal of peripheral friends is actually a blessing in disguise. I really do not have the strength or time to worry about them.

*

M.G. COY
Myrton's 56-year-old wife Maureen
died of heart failure in 2012

Maureen's family is from Somerville, Massachusetts, and they have distanced themselves from me. They do not want any of her things, and seem not to want to help me dispose of them. I set up a scholarship at the high school where Maureen worked, but they do not want to help. My wife loved and helped many children when she was there. Her only daughter, who doctors had said she could never have, has taken her loss badly. As for me, after four years I am still struggling with the sudden loss.

*

BILL DOWNS
Bill's 21-year-old son Brad and 19-year-old daughter-in-law
Samantha were killed by a drunk driver in 2007

When my kids were killed, the grief and sorrow made me feel overwhelmed. After days of self-persecution, my marriage began to suffer. On October 22, 2011, I told Julie I did not love her any more.

I was so out of my mind with grief, and hate for God, that I couldn't see loving anyone, including my wife. I guess I figured if I couldn't get back at God any other way, I would use Julie to hurt Him. For a year and two months I gave Julie hell. I verbally treated her like crap. I never physically hurt her, but the mental abuse I was giving her was more than any woman should have to put up with.

On December 6, 2012, it all came to a head. Julie never gave up praying, but enough was enough. She told me to get out. Luckily, her prayers were answered, because she never actually gave up on me. She always kept praying for me even though I did not deserve the time of day. Our families never knew the depth of the problems we were having, but knowing the surface of it was bad enough. They gave up on me a long time before Julie did. But her love and her prayers held out until the end. When I finally came to my senses, we went to counseling and were able to reunite our love.

The next day, on December 7, I gave my heart to Christ and on February 9, 2013, Julie and I renewed our vows. She rededicated her life to Christ and I was baptized on profession of faith. But for the first time, I felt I had actually given my life to God. Now Julie and I spend every day together and build the love we have for each other by living our lives for God, for each other and for our kids.

*

JAMES FENNELL
James' 21-year-old daughter Lauren
was killed by a drunk driver in 2008

Nine short months after the loss of my daughter, my wife of twenty-eight years asked for a divorce. In an eighteen-month period, I had experienced the loss of my father, my daughter, my mother, and then finally my marriage.

Grief is a very personal journey. Everyone proceeds with grief at his or her own pace. Almost never does a couple move through grief at the same pace or in the same manner. Perhaps the most difficult types of problems a couple can encounter occur when one spouse shuts down or refuses to speak to the other half about the child, or about the problems that he or she may be having, or turns to excessive drinking or drugs to masquerade the problem. I would like to say to anyone who perceives that drinking or the use of drugs eases the pain, that perception could not be farther from the truth. The grief is still there waiting for him, because he hasn't done anything to move through that grief.

If one partner navigates through grief more successfully than the other, it is important for the other partner not to think that moving through the grieving process is showing disrespect for the child. Often this uneven movement through grief causes the breakup of a marriage, as it did in my case. The most important thing to remember is that our children want us to have a happy and meaningful life.

In August 2009, I moved from my home state of New York to southern New Jersey in order to be closer to my surviving daughter, Amanda, who had just started school in Maryland. In addition, I had no remaining family in New York; they had either moved or had passed on. I started a new life and embraced this new beginning as an opportunity to move on in a positive manner.

*

JEFF GARDNER
Jeff's 18-year-old daughter Cassidy
was killed by a drugged driver in 2013

I don't believe it has impacted any of my relationships in a negative way. Sometimes I feel like I get irritated more often, and am not the best company to be around, but I think my family is closer than we were before losing Cassidy. We definitely don't take a day, or each other, for granted, and always try to make memories together because, in the end, memories are all we have.

*

MICHAEL GERSHE
Mike was 8 weeks old when his 28-year-old mom
Barbara was killed by a drunk driver in 1970
Mike was 33 when his 33-year-old best friend John
was killed in a drunk driving crash in 2004

I did not have any relationships strained by the death of my mother within my family or friends. The only thing I wish I had done differently was to not be afraid to be in a relationship when I was younger, or even now. I'm scared of going through what my father went through with the loss of his wife and mother of his kids. Although I date, I can be emotionally distant with a wall between me and the woman. I do not want her to see the the pain, maybe because I don't want to seem like a wounded person and need fixing. Letting someone through that wall is tough, and I wish it could be easy to let it down at times. I know women want men to open up, but it just scares the crap out of us to do so; at least it does for me.

With John's death, I don't think any relationship was impacted negatively as a group. I believe that if anything, the circle of friends became even stronger. John had a unique ability to bring people together, and that is what happened with his death. I can recall after the wake filling his house with people looking at pictures and just telling Big John stories. We all loved the guy, and if anyone needed someone, we were there for him or her.

*

CARL HARMS
Carl's mother Myrtle died from malpractice in 2005
Carl's 56-year-old father James was killed by a drunk driver in 2007

In the beginning, my family understood and provided comfort.

153

But as the hours and days went on, they became distant from my pain. They then grew very frustrated with me because I wouldn't simply move on, and my number one priority was making sure my father's death didn't go unnoticed, and that someone should answer for it. Now, nine years later, I still remember, I still cry, I still wish. But I fight for peace. I've lost some friends due to their lack of compassion or understanding of my new world and why I fight. Most of them simply don't want to accept the world as I now see it, and would simply prefer to forget that it ever happened. As time has passed, folks have accepted the new world I live in, and know that there is nothing they can do to fix it. And, as for those who can't, I was blessed to know them and they will always be part of my life even if they don't want to be part of mine.

*

STEPHEN HOCHHAUS
Stephen's 51-year-old wife Kathy
died from adult soft tissue sarcoma in 2011

My friends have stuck by me in my loss and I will always be grateful for that. One friend did, however, suggest I date and find a new relationship within four months of my wife's death. I forgive him for that, because he has never known the deep love like I have. He has never married, and lives a life quite different from mine. His suggestions ended when he realized that it wasn't going to happen.

I developed a close friendship with my wife's best friend, who supports my feelings and gives me a great deal of comfort when we can talk about Kathy together. Her own grief is not lost to me either. I also became closer to a customer of mine whose husband I had known and who had died seventeen years earlier. This lady understood the pain I was feeling, since she had known Kathy, and we began going to dinner and talking about our mutual loss. I was drawn to her because she never married again, having found the love of her life, and more important, she kept on living. She started doing things on her own such as learning to paint and traveling. She became a mentor to me and helped me to see that I could indeed keep on living. She told me there will be days when you will still cry, for it never truly ends, but you will keep going.

Some of my family members, however, caused me severe anguish. My brother, who always could create tension and stress in my life, told me in me in my own home, in so many words, that he was tired of hearing about my wife. That was five months after Kathy died, not to mention the fact that we had very limited contact as it was. We have not spoken since. My sister-in-law did even worse. From the day of my wife's death, she was inquiring about a will and wanted to know about property that Kathy and I owned. She said this to me just after I left the funeral home. It went downhill after that. She always had a way of making my wife upset and cry. Kathy always forgave her, saying, "But she's my sister." I cannot excuse her behavior so easily. So after Kathy's parents passed, within two years after her, I lost contact with her sister. I have never been one to burn bridges, yet I also know that anything I could ever say to either my brother or sister-in-law would only fall on deaf ears.

*

DAVID JONES
David's 54-year-old wife Judy
was killed by a drunk driver in 2008

I think the relationship with my children has been the most impacted by Judy's death. I still maintain as close relationships as I can, but Judy was very close to our children, and my deciding to remarry took a long time to build acceptance between them and my new wife, Diane. Diane and I took two years from when we started seeing each other before marrying. All our children, their spouses, and grandchildren were part of the wedding instead of having a maid of honor and best man.

*

JOHN PETE
John's 71-year-old grandmother Tita died
from diabetes and a series of strokes in 1989

I learned long ago that other people tire of your grief and losses long before you are ready to stop talking about them. I have supportive family members and friends, but there have also been letdowns when I needed support for losses and grief. It's always a good idea to have a broad base of supportive people and other resources.

*

ROBERT RIECK
Robert's 18-year-old daughter
Ashley died by suicide in 2016

The journey has definitely affected my relationships. First and foremost was the relationship with my wife. The blame from one spouse to the other pretty much began right away. No matter how hard I tried to think in an open-minded way, the honesty of the situation smacked me in the face. I had to make the ultimate decision to end my marriage of almost twenty-three years. I had also decided that a friend who I had previously thought was my closest friend was not there for me, and I ended it. I have not been close to my mother after my brother's death and after she did not even bother to come to my daughter's funeral. Our relationship has worsened, and I haven't talked to her since Ashley's death.

*

CHAPTER TWELVE

THE FAITH

Love is the only law capable of transforming grief into hope. -LYNDA CHELDELIN FELL

Grief has far-reaching effects in most areas of our life, including faith. For some, our faith can deepen as it becomes a safe haven for our sorrow. For others, it can be a source of disappointment, leading to fractured beliefs. How has your faith been impacted by your loss?

*

CHUCK ANDREAS
Chuck's 60-year-old wife Gloria
died unexpectedly from heart disease in 2014

I come from an Irish Catholic family, so yes, faith has been a source of comfort. My faith has been strengthened because of my need to be reunited with Glor. I pray every night, and as I've stated before, every morning when I take the dog out I always say "Good morning, Glor." On a lighter note, I was telling my sister Kimmy I was praying more, and she said good, that it would make my late mom happy.

*

JEFF BALDWIN
Jeff's 20-year-old son Matthew died
in a drowning accident in 2011

I never questioned God when I lost my son Matthew. I was confused, and wondered why this was happening to me. However, my faith only grew stronger. A very personal story, one that I have never shared with anyone except my partner, happened to me three days after my son had passed. I was at home alone and trying to edit together a celebration of life video of my son's life in photos and video clips that would be played at the chapel service the next day. I was praying all that day and I asked God to show me or reveal to me something that would help me make sense of what had happened. At that exact time while I was sitting there taking a break from piecing together this video, my body went numb and I could feel the Holy Spirit coming over me. I could feel a beam of light, like rays of sunshine on my face. I was surprised at first and a little scared, however that all went away when God started laying these things on my heart.

The best way I can explain it with accuracy is that God was showing me these images of my son. First it showed my son's addiction and experimenting with drugs getting worse to the point that his life was in a full downward spiral. At this point I prayed to God and said out loud, "Please, dear God, please show me more," and the images continued. It showed my son getting deeper and deeper into his addiction. He was, at this point in the images, just sleeping on friends' couches, anywhere he could find a place to crash. The last image was the hardest image to see. It showed that my son had frozen to death in an alley between two businesses. He had been using drugs and drinking alcohol, and was trying to find shelter in the early morning hours. It appeared to be a cold night, and the images revealed that Matthew died from hypothermia.

God laid on my heart and reminded me that all my adult life, ever since I had kids, I had always prayed at night for him to watch over my children, and to keep them safe and protected. So why would I be shown these images, and the way they played out? That was revealed to me as well.

As much as I loved my son and daughter, I could only advise Matthew and try to help him, but I could not live his life for him. God spared me from seeing what would have been the slow demise of my son slowly killing himself with the drug use and alcohol. My son was at that under-age party, and sometime in the early morning hours of July 29, 2011, he slipped below the water's surface and woke up in God's arms in heaven. The images revealed to me what would have taken place, and how Matt would have died. It made perfect sense after the images were revealed to me. I felt honored, and still do, that God allowed me to see these images, and it greatly helped me to accept things, and I didn't need to question them.

I still grieve deeply for my son; however, I have that assurance in the back of my mind that Matt is with God in heaven and his spiritual life continues, and one day I will see him again.

*

ROBERT BOOS
Robert's 21-year-old son Kevin
was killed by a drunk driver in 2015

It started a long time ago when I was a good Catholic boy who went to church every weekend or so and even went to some week-long novenas that my grandmother used to drag me to. Then my mother got divorced in the 1970s and the church effectively banned her. Then there were the abuse scandals of the church. I was pretty much done with organized religion from that point forward.

My ex-wife, Kevin's mother, was always very religious and very involved with the Catholic faith. All three of our children went to Catholic school. They participated in Sunday school, first communion, confirmation, and all of that. Kevin did not like it at all. He was very vocal in his opposition to participating in any of it. He had a specific problem with a Sunday school teacher who drove him away from the church as well. As soon as the kids turned eighteen, their participation with any religious activities or services was few and far between.

I connect almost daily with a group of over two thousand people who have lost children in an online group. There are many in this group who are of deep faith and claim that it has helped them tremendously. But there are many who say that this loss has driven a wedge between themselves and religion and God. There are some who outright hate God for allowing this to happen.

I believe in a higher being. I think there is too much beauty and purpose in this world for there not to be a God. What I resist is the Catholics, or any religious order for that matter, saying there is only one true religion, that what they do is the only right way and what God would want. There are probably a billion followers of other faiths who would say the same about the Catholics, the Jews or the Christians. Who am I to say who is right or wrong?

However this god form manifests in my or anyone's life, I am indeed wondering about his participation in the death of my son. Or, at the very least his intervention at the time my son was killed. How does a loving God allow three beautiful people in the prime of life to be taken from us so completely and suddenly? Then again, this is the same God who allows parents to lose babies at childbirth (or before), for little children to suffer and die from a horrible cancer, or even a child's heart to stop suddenly in their sleep.

How many times do you hear, "My child was in an accident, but Jesus protected him." I have heard this. So if Jesus does exist and he really is the Son of God, and he really can save people, what exactly was he doing at 9:15 p.m. on September 6, 2015? I'm sure there are a lot of things going on, but these were three amazing people and three very selfless people. They weren't bad people. If there was ever a time Jesus or God, or any form of supreme being, should have intervened, this was it.

One particularly brutal comment just popped into my mind as I write this. It was a day or two after the death of these three wonderful kids, and I was looking at some of the Facebook posts. I probably shouldn't have. The grandmother of one of the kids' friends in Tallahassee, who wasn't in the car, posted on one of the main threads about the deaths, "Thank God my grandson wasn't in that car! God is so good!" Seriously, she said that. My first thought was, what does God have to do with this? Why would God save your good kid (which he is), and allow my good kid and my other two friends' good kids to be killed?

I hope there is a God. I hope he knows what a good person I am, and that if there is a time to judge, He sees all. I hope He would see through all of this.

*

M.G. COY
Myrton's 56-year-old wife Maureen
died of heart failure in 2012

Yes. My faith has been a challenge right now!

161

*

BILL DOWNS
Bill's 21-year-old son Brad and 19-year-old daughter-in-law
Samantha were killed by a drunk driver in 2007

My faith died when the kids died. Our pastor at the time was very supportive, and through the whole grieving process he was there for me. It was his devotion to our faith that helped me process my grief and regain my faith in God. I never lost sight of the beliefs of my faith, but just lost my personal faith. Once I regained my faith in God, my faith belief gave me comfort. There is no doubt in my heart where our kids are at. I know that they are sleeping until Jesus calls us all home.

*

JAMES FENNELL
James' 21-year-old daughter Lauren
was killed by a drunk driver in 2008

I just couldn't reconcile the God that religion introduced me to with someone who would allow such suffering. The church and the priests I spoke to were of absolutely no help. I had been raised a Roman Catholic and considered myself a devout member of that religion for my entire life. Eventually, through much pain and anguish and inner turmoil, I came to realize that the God I had been taught about was largely a fabrication of man. Consequently, I became free of religion altogether and took my own journey, led not by priests but by my inner self on a journey of discovery.

What I came to discover through reading many of the writings of spiritual teachers far surpassed anything a priest, a religion or a church could possibly offer. I began to envision that religion, particularly the church, teaches us to focus our attention on it, instead of within. This self-awareness led me in a different direction. I discovered that we are all truly a divine spark of this being we refer to as God. He has embedded every single one of us with the ability to progress our souls. I learned that our time here is to grow and move forward beyond our present experience onto greater things, and our consciousness has to expand and evolve in order to be able to function on the next level of being.

Ultimately, as the years passed, I came to the realization that so many people have discovered spiritual growth *only* through the trauma they have experienced. I started to grasp the belief that my daughter came here to give me this experience in order to awaken me. We, as eternal beings, I was to learn, are intimately involved in helping our loved ones progress our souls, and it is our love which is our unending connection.

*

JEFF GARDNER
Jeff's 18-year-old daughter Cassidy
was killed by a drugged driver in 2013

I definitely believe God has His will. Sometimes it's not our will, but He gave the ultimate gift so I can spend eternity with her and the rest of my loved ones.

*

MICHAEL GERSHE
Mike was 8 weeks old when his 28-year-old mom
Barbara was killed by a drunk driver in 1970
Mike was 33 when his 33-year-old best friend John
was killed in a drunk driving crash in 2004

I've been angry at God most of my adult life. I've questioned Him and cursed Him for taking my mother away from me, as well as my brother, my father, and my mother's family. She was a young mother, only twenty-eight and a schoolteacher. Why did He have to take her? For what purpose?! Perhaps my being mad at Him is why I am not such a devoted Jew, now that I think about it. I have so many questions that will never be answered, and that drives me insane when it comes to faith.

While I really believe I live my life with strong Jewish principles, I can't always find comfort in my own religion. It's definitely an internal struggle to find that peace. I know God is not responsible for killing my mother and that a drunk driver is, but we usually look toward a higher power, or believe that there is a higher power who does things for a reason.

My faith was already negatively impacted before John's death as I tried to cope with my mother's death. I don't think it got any better. I would ask, "Why John?" at times. I believe I will always have a love-hate relationship with God, but I never sought out faith to help me get through John's death. I would rather have the support of my friends or family, to be honest.

*

CARL HARMS
Carl's mother Myrtle died from malpractice in 2005
Carl's 56-year-old father James was killed by a drunk driver in 2007

My faith was strained before my father's death, because we were still freshly on the heels of the sudden death of my mother. I questioned God and asked what I had done that deserved such darkness. In the immediate days following, folks made the mistake of saying certain things that would lead me to lean away from my faith. My faith is in a God who cries as I cry, and smiles as I smile. My image of God is a comforting one of a majestic homecoming in his loving arms, not of a God who people think would allow these tragic events to take place without stopping it. It wasn't God's will that my father be violently thrown into the windshield, then ripped backward out of his pants, tangled in the seatbelt and crushed in the back seat. That wasn't God's will, it was man's will that allowed this to happen.

If you value those you love, then please do not try to comfort them by saying, "God needed more angels, so he took your father," "It was his time," etc. I don't want the thought that my God, my loving God, had anything to do with this, and if it weren't for the selfish acts of man I would still hear my father's contagious laughter. My faith was tested, but it has grown stronger in the belief that God was there for my father when a man killed him. If you fear the questioning of God's purpose or existence, then your heart is in the right place and it will regain the faith needed to believe in love.

*

STEPHEN HOCHHAUS
Stephen's 51-year-old wife Kathy
died from adult soft tissue sarcoma in 2011

My wife and I were not very religious, although I was raised that way. Every time I looked at her, I was able to see that a person could be the most kind, forgiving, helpful soul with no room for hate in his or her heart. When my mom died, I was thirty years old. I prayed so hard that God would save her life. He didn't. My wife always said that if things were meant to happen, they will. When the doctors told me Kathy had five days to live, I had to tell her myself. Kathy simply said, "It is what it is." That was her simple philosophy. She never shed a tear or asked "Why me?" She just left. She and I totally believed in fate. She told me just before she died that she would find a way to reach me if she possibly could. She found a way, big time. To have faith is to believe in something that cannot be proven. To have faith is to believe in something that cannot be touched, smelled, heard, felt, or seen. Fate, you see, can only be experienced only if you have faith. That has become my simple philosophy.

*

DAVID JONES
David's 54-year-old wife Judy
was killed by a drunk driver in 2008

My faith in God has actually deepened since Judy's death. She was my spiritual mentor, and I treasure her notes and writings and the few recordings I have of her sermons. When she died, the book she had with her in the car was *Spiritual Direction: Wisdom for the Long Walk of Faith,* by Henri Nouwen, and her blood was all over the cover. It was a library book, so I just paid for the book and continue to use it for spiritual guidance.

At the time she died, I don't think she could have been closer to God than she was. There were countless sticky notes for people she was praying for, as well as research for future sermon topics and church planning. She was a source of spiritual comfort and guidance for many women in our church, and one of my regrets is all the people she would have helped in the future had she not died then. It was extremely hard for me to be in church over the first couple of years and see all the roles she used to fill now being done by other people. It just made me cry over and over.

After Judy died, I served on our church's finance committee for the next six years. One reason for this was to see through the projects she had planned for children's ministry, and to do what I could to help bring those projects to fruition. Many people donated money in Judy's name to provide funding for creating a children's church, an area where four to six-year-olds could worship in an age-appropriate way. I led this group and was part of the team leading Children's Church for the next five years after her death. I tried to channel her vision for continuing to serve children. I also helped with the puppet ministry, replacing Judy, and have become a regular puppeteer for the little kids.

This morning I visited Judy's grave, watered the flowers, and had a long talk with God. It was eight years ago today that Judy died, and I needed some comfort. I thanked him for every minute I had with her, and prayed that someday we would be reunited in Heaven.

I remember a dream I had about six months after she died. I had been driving on twisty rural roads in mountains and hills for a long time when I came to a valley where Judy was preaching to villagers. She told me she had been assigned a mission from God, and that I needed to stop looking for her every night in my dreams and let her go. I will never forget her, but I also had to rebuild my life without her physical presence.

My faith in God is why I continue to do victim impact presentations to DUI offenders. I try to save lives and continue Judy's ministry, extending her legacy.

*

JOHN PETE
John's 71-year-old grandmother Tita died
from diabetes and a series of strokes in 1989

Faith has been a big part of my journey with very difficult losses, and I have grown spiritually from that challenge. Faith during losses is an interesting thing. Earlier in life I found myself turning my back on God in anger. But that did not work out well for me, because it added an even bigger gap in addition to the absence of loved one who had died.

I have concluded that there is a very real choice: to lean away from or onto God. And leaning onto God has given me courage, strength, peace, acceptance and renewed hope.

*

ROBERT RIECK
Robert's 18-year-old daughter
Ashley died by suicide in 2016

I suppose my faith has been impacted as a result of Ashley's death. I could not understand why a god would take someone so precious in my life and let her suffer, and cause all of us to suffer. It has been tough to even go to church. I tried a few months later, but just could not do it.

*

CHAPTER THIRTEEN

THE INTIMACY

Physical intimacy isn't and can never be an
effective substitute for emotional intimacy.
-JOHN GREEN

Following loss, it's hard to get excited about anything, including
intimacy. For some, the change in sexual intimacy is brief and lasts
for only a short time. For others it can be longer-lasting and place
an even greater strain on already fragile emotions. Has your loss
affected your ability to enjoy intimacy?

*

CHUCK ANDREAS
Chuck's 60-year-old wife Gloria
died unexpectedly from heart disease in 2014

My loss has definitely affected my ability to enjoy intimacy,
because being with someone else right now is the farthest thing
from my mind. I am still having a hard time trying to understand
what happened. I understand that it's a debate, but losing someone
unexpectedly and knowing someone is passing away are two
completely different mindsets. My friend who lost his wife to
cancer cannot understand why I am not looking for a relationship.
Right now, at this point in time if I started a relationship with

someone, it would almost feel like I was cheating. I loved my wife the way you see in movies or read about in books. We did everything together, we never went out alone, because we wanted it that way. We had that nonverbal communication where we could just look at each other and understand what the other was thinking. We enjoyed the same things, which I cannot imagine being able to do with someone else. Like our wedding song said, "Until the mountains crumble to the sea, there will always be you and me." Look, I am going to be honest and say I have no clue as to what's ahead. If I don't ever have a relationship again, so be it. I was lucky enough once.

*

JEFF BALDWIN
Jeff's 20-year-old son Matthew died
in a drowning accident in 2011

Before the loss of my son I was being treated for chronic back pain from previous injuries to the lower back. I was prescribed pain pills to help. After the loss of my son I freely admit that I started taking more pills daily to help ease or mask the pain that I was dealing with. This went on for over a year before I got help. It's so easy to turn to something else in order to escape reality and the pain. This journey of grief is not easy; however, over time you learn new ways of coping with your loss and pain, and you can be there for others who are new to this grief journey. I choose to spend my time around work and life by running a support group on Facebook called Mending Hearts Grief support group, and also being affiliated with other groups in helping others.

*

ROBERT BOOS
Robert's 21-year-old son Kevin
was killed by a drunk driver in 2015

I have certainly withdrawn in a lot of situations of friendship and family moments. I just feel like I do not have the strength or the tolerance to deal with some situations. But intimacy? I have not experienced any issues in this area. I can certainly understand where this could be really impacted in this situation, but thankfully I'm not a textbook case in this matter.

*

RODNEY CLOUTIER
Rodney's 21-year-old fiancéee Cattie was killed by a drunk
driver in 2013, and his premature daughter Dottie died in 2016

The loss of our daughter did affect our intimacy for a little while on her end, but eventually it went away.

*

M.G. COY
Myrton's 56-year-old wife Maureen
died of heart failure in 2012

Intimacy, what is that? I have no desire for it after spending thirty-five years with the love of my life. My therapist wants me to socialize more. I am slowly trying to get there. It is not easy for me, but I think I will get there in time. I have not given up hope. I have been in customer service most of my life. I like people and try to be kind. Always.

*

BILL DOWNS
Bill's 21-year-old son Brad and 19-year-old daughter-in-law
Samantha were killed by a drunk driver in 2007

For a long time my guilt kept me from any type of closeness to my wife. My only thought at that time was that I could not protect my kids from this tragedy. My wife was my only link to the kids. We were lucky; her faith in me and in our love kept us from losing each other. Our desire to seek help from counseling for our marriage and faith in God helped us to start over and to close the gap that my grief had developed.

*

JAMES FENNELL
James' 21-year-old daughter Lauren
was killed by a drunk driver in 2008

Intimacy in my relationship came to a complete halt. It is something that can be recovered only if both parties are concerned about it and if both desire to address any issues which may be preventing a solution. I have always felt that two-way communication is the most effective tool to address such issues, and when communication becomes a one-way street it is impossible to successfully address the issue, or any other issue for that matter.

*

MICHAEL GERSHE
Mike was 8 weeks old when his 28-year-old mom
Barbara was killed by a drunk driver in 1970
Mike was 33 when his 33-year-old best friend John
was killed in a drunk driving crash in 2004

I think the death of my mother does affect my ability to enjoy intimacy on the mental aspect of a relationship, since I hide behind humor. I think that as men we deflect our feelings because we learn that society wants strong men who can handle anything. But behind closed doors we fall apart and never want anyone to see the pain. I do think I am fragile and wear my emotions on my sleeve, but I often use my humor to block true intimacy in my relationships. What is weird is that I can stand on stage and open my soul to an audience full of strangers. But with someone I may care about, I feel too vulnerable to do the same. I am not sure what I am so afraid of, because if the other person really cares about me, then opening up and showing my true emotions, my anger, my hurt will only bring us together. I guess it's easier said than done.

I don't think John's loss affected my ability to enjoy intimacy as much as the death of my mother did. I think I open up more about John with someone and what his death meant to me. He was one of my best friends, and if he were alive I would want that person to definitely know him. I get sad when I talk about him, because there are fifteen years of memories to cope with. But I don't think it affects my ability to enjoy intimacy with someone. Of course, as a man, I am probably in denial or don't even realize that it does impact intimacy, so you may have to ask someone I've dated. Wait, on second thought, perhaps not...

*

STEPHEN HOCHHAUS
Stephen's 51-year-old wife Kathy
died from adult soft tissue sarcoma in 2011

I was raised in a loving family with a lot of display of affection. My parents were always hugging and kissing. It was who they were, and I believe why I became the same.

When I think about the most intimate moments I shared with my wife, it wasn't the sex that comes to mind first, which of course was the greatest. Rather, it was those times when I would nuzzle my nose in her neck while she was putting on her makeup before we would go out. She might have called me a pest, but she knew what it meant. She knew it was her that I wanted. That is something I can never have again, for it is way too personal, too intimate.

My loss has destroyed any desire to be intimate with another woman. I just cannot rid myself of feelings or thoughts about the woman I still love, and I cannot separate sex from love. Sex without emotional intimacy holds no interest for me. For me it's just wrong. Kathy told me that if I needed to be with someone it would be okay. She knew better than to suggest that I find another love, for we both knew I was a done deal. But I did ponder it, and quickly came to the realization that it was not a place I wanted to go. Were I a young man I might feel differently, but I'm sixty-seven and I'm fortunate enough to have my need for hugs and kisses met by my dear grandchildren.

We are all different, and our grief is our own. How we deal with our needs and desires is also unique to us. The worst thing we can do is judge ourselves or others for how we choose to live the remainder of our lives. For once you become widowed, you are kind of on your own. You want to be true to yourself and your own feelings and needs, and you must.

*

DAVID JONES
David's 54-year-old wife Judy
was killed by a drunk driver in 2008

Judy was a superb teacher in this aspect of life. Each relationship will have its own special dynamics; no two are the same, but each can be appreciated to its fullest if both partners respect each other and show love in every little action.

Great relationships require regular intimacy, having both sides fully committed, and also having something extra to give a spark and keep things fresh. Each person is constantly thinking of the other and looking for little ways to show love and affection.

Judy and I had every Saturday night as a "Mom and Dad" night. The kids would be upstairs watching DVDs and having pizza and popcorn while we would watch a romantic comedy downstairs, and then I would make dinner, grilling steaks, halibut, or kabobs, with baked potatoes or rice and a vegetable like green beans, carrots, or asparagus. We had a café table with two chairs in an alcove of our bedroom with a tablecloth, candles, flowers, and champagne or cranberry juice. We would have a romantic candlelight dinner with music and just enjoy each other's company. We would talk about the past, plan for the future and enjoy the moment. Friday night was always family night so that the kids would respect Saturday as our night. Judy cooked during the week and I would cook on Saturday night.

With my present wife, Diane, we have kids and grandkids over on a regular basis and have about half our nights with just the two of us. We take turns cooking and dine out about every third time. Diane is great at keeping things fresh, and I never know what surprise she has in store next.

*

JOHN PETE
John's 71-year-old grandmother Tita died
from diabetes and a series of strokes in 1989

Loss absolutely poses complicated challenges with personal relationships. When your heart hurts badly, intimacy may be the last thing you are interested in as you struggle to cope with the implications of your loss.

The people closest to you are sometimes trying hard to comfort you at a time when you may need more personal space, and that can be interpreted as rejection. It also happens in reverse.

A helpful dynamic is one where you can express your grief needs openly to family and friends. It doesn't work perfectly, but it's important to communicate your changing needs so others know what those needs are and can better support you.

*

ROBERT RIECK
Robert's 18-year-old daughter
Ashley died by suicide in 2016

Intimacy has been nonexistent. It was already that way before Ashley died, but it definitely made it impossible afterward.

*

CHAPTER FOURTEEN

THE STEREOTYPE

I speak the truth not so much as I would, but as much as I dare. And I dare a little more as I grow older. -MICHEL DE MONTAIGNE

She cries, he sighs. This is a stereotype held by many: that women view themselves as more expressive and intuitive, while men don't ever want to talk about their feelings. The truth is that grief isn't one-size-fits-all. But gender differences aside, what do you want women to know about your emotions in relation to loss? What is the hardest emotion for you to express?

*

CHUCK ANDREAS
Chuck's 60-year-old wife Gloria
died unexpectedly from heart disease in 2014

There really is nothing that jumps out at me about my emotions that I would like women to know, except what they already know, and that is that I don't discuss my feelings with everyone. There are a limited number of people I discuss them with to go beyond the generic answer "I'm doing all right." Please understand, it is nothing personal. I just don't discuss my actual feelings with everyone. The hardest emotion for me to express is how much pain

177

I'm really in. It is easier for me to shut myself in my house and deal with it alone than it is to discuss it. I guess I was brought up old school, and it wasn't just my parents, it was also friends in my early adulthood. With my friends, if you had a problem you had to deal with it yourself and move on. Believe me, it drives me crazy sometimes, because I am willing to help anyone, but when it comes to me, I try to deal with it alone.

*

JEFF BALDWIN
Jeff's 20-year-old son Matthew died
in a drowning accident in 2011

The hardest thing for me to express is the reasoning behind how my son died in an aboveground swimming pool when he was a perfect swimmer. He didn't have a heart attack or anything like that. He was drinking at the party, and the partygoers were experimenting with these prescription drugs that each kid brought, without knowing the strength of each medication or its use. That is what led to my son's losing consciousness. I explain to people whom he didn't know that his actions that night and early the next morning would end up robbing him of life. He simply went unconscious and went to sleep and woke up in God's arms.

*

ROBERT BOOS
Robert's 21-year-old son Kevin
was killed by a drunk driver in 2015

I am a typical male in that I do not openly express my feelings well, or perhaps not at all. I was very embarrassed at showing my emotions in the first days after my son's death; which is completely insane to feel that way, but yet I was. I completely lost it when I first saw my brother and my mother, and then again when I saw my friend Rob, who lost his son in the same crash. I think back about that and I feel embarrassment about it. There is probably not one person who saw any of that reaction who would be embarrassed for me or think that I was embarrassed, but I was.

Since then I have not let anyone see very much emotion from me. To anyone who sees me, I am the picture of calm and at peace. But inside, in that place that nobody sees (until they read this), my emotions are wildly swinging, even a year later. The inner turmoil that I feel and the barrage of emotions of loss and pain are paralyzing at times. But to see me or relate with me in a work situation, a family situation or a friendship situation, you wouldn't know it. You might even think I've gotten over it or moved on after this horrible loss. That could not be farther from the truth. I'm as devastated and upset as I was the day of the loss. I just don't let you know it.

The best place I've found to express my feelings and thoughts is on The Compassionate Friends closed Facebook group "TCF – Loss of a Child." On that website, I am able to privately share some of my saddest moments and even some horrible thoughts with a group of moms and dads who have lost exactly what I have and understand what I'm talking about. The group currently has just over two thousand people and is an absolute godsend. I have also been able to help people who have come after me and offer my words of wisdom to help them. This has been a major help to me, the ability to help others. You also find out that when you lose a child you gain a "death pass" where you can openly talk to others about their loss, because you are in the group. A conversation I never would have had with someone who has lost a child becomes commonplace in the hope that sharing is helping.

I mean this as no slight to those who have fortunately not lost a child. They just don't get it. When you can start a conversation with me, "I cannot imagine....," then how could you possibly understand? When you talk to a parent who is farther along in this grief journey than you are, or you are trying to help a new member who has just lost a child and is very raw in his or her grief, you feel like a viable member of that community. You feel like you belong to this group, can offer opinions very openly, and also ask questions about a mother or father's precious child who was lost. You can ask questions that a nonmember would find very difficult to ask. You will also find that you gain comfort from others, and that you also can provide comfort to others at this horrible time just by stating how you feel and what, if anything, has made you feel better.

What I have learned from other men (and myself) is that we take the responsibility for being the protector very seriously. Many of us (me included) feel like we have failed miserably with the loss of our child. We get deeply caught up in the "what if" game — what if I had done this or what if I had done that, would my child still be alive? That tears most of us up significantly. We also believe we retain the protector role over our surviving children, spouses or significant others, and family. Showing any kind of emotion or weakness is not allowed. We have to be strong for all of the remaining friends and family.

*

RODNEY CLOUTIER
Rodney's 21-year-old fiancéee Cattie was killed by a drunk
driver in 2013, and his premature daughter Dottie died in 2016

We men don't show any grieving signs; we do it in our own ways. Constantly asking us only irritates us. When we're ready, we will say something. As for the ones who do show it a lot, I can't help you there. I'm more the quiet kind.

*

M.G. COY
Myrton's 56-year-old wife Maureen
died of heart failure in 2012

I need someone to understand that my emotions are widely confusing for me. I have never been in this type of situation in my life. Dealing with it has been a struggle for me. I am now trying to sell my home to downsize to a condo. Very difficult, but I am trying to move forward. I am looking for some happiness in my life.

*

BILL DOWNS
Bill's 21-year-old son Brad and 19-year-old daughter-in-law
Samantha were killed by a drunk driver in 2007

Call it ego or call it instinct: man's will to protect his wife and family is the utmost desire in his heart. To do this, a man feels he must sacrifice his own feelings to protect his family, his wife. The hardest emotion I have had to express is the pain I felt when my kids died. Losing them because of an impaired driver was a horrific blow to my ego, to the protection I was supposed to give to my family. I was taught that a man should never cry. I had to stay strong for my wife, when in reality I was dying inside. I have learned that a real man does cry. Doing so does not make him less of a man. The one thing that made me realize it was okay to cry was when I read John 11:35 in the Bible. It's the shortest of all verses in the Bible: "Jesus wept." When I read those two words in the Bible, I realized that real men cry. It is okay to show your emotions, men. Wives, comfort your man. We hurt too, even if we are too proud to admit it.

*

JAMES FENNELL
James' 21-year-old daughter Lauren
was killed by a drunk driver in 2008

I have never had a difficult time expressing emotions. I found that the more I conversed with other bereaved parents and/or professional counselors, the more I began to heal. Women need to sometimes become aware that a father's loss cuts as deep as a mother's. It is only society's mores that prohibit the man from displaying the same emotions that women are often freer than men to express.

*

MICHAEL GERSHE
Mike was 8 weeks old when his 28-year-old mom
Barbara was killed by a drunk driver in 1970
Mike was 33 when his 33-year-old best friend John
was killed in a drunk driving crash in 2004

I would like women to know that men are emotional and we do cry, and not just when our team wins a championship. The hardest part is actually expressing ourselves to women because we just don't want to be seen as weak, or at least that is how I see it. Men, by society's rules, are supposed to be tough. We may want to share our feelings, but just don't know how. Perhaps I have a different situation, because my mother died when I was so young, and it's hard for me since I have no memories of her. I grieve her death even though I didn't know her.

Opening up is not something we are used to or comfortable with, but we will, in our own timeframe. You can't rush us or we will never open up to you with our emotions when it comes to our grief journey. Perhaps it is a pride thing too, and we think we can handle it ourselves, when in truth we really cannot. The hardest emotion for me to express is probably the pain I feel because I protect myself so much. I end up keeping myself at a distance so I don't feel that pain of losing someone like my father did with my mother. It's a rotten way to live, even when I am in a relationship, because I don't allow myself to feel loved. Even though I know I should let the wall down for someone, I guess it's just much easier said than done.

Big John's death left a huge gap in my life, just like it did for everyone who knew him. The people we are close with are like family, and that is how he was to everyone, like someone's brother. My grief journey has not been easy, and I think we men find ways to cope that work for us. We probably won't volunteer our feelings, but that doesn't mean we aren't hurting. We will withdraw, we use our humor, sometimes inappropriately as a defense mechanism. We will spend hours in the garage or man cave alone with our thoughts. We have the same emotions as women, but we also feel that we have to remain strong at the same time. It's tough to ask for help when we need it too; at least it is in my case. I feel like I need to handle it on my own, which is probably farther than the truth after writing about it.

*

STEPHEN HOCHHAUS
Stephen's 51-year-old wife Kathy
died from adult soft tissue sarcoma in 2011

I experienced firsthand the difference between how men and women react when they have lost someone they love. I never gave it much thought until I looked back on my own grief journey. From the moment my wife died, I said to myself, "You're a man. You can handle this." I walked away from that hospice home where my wife left me, knowing I had a job to do. There were funeral arrangements to make and a business to keep going. I was contacted by the hospice organization to take advantage of grief counseling and support groups that they offered. I received phone calls and letters telling me that they were there to help. I was a man! I could make it. For two months I kept myself going as if I were under control, only to collapse on my kitchen floor in a pool of emotion. I had to make the call, if only to save my own life. The next day a grief counselor was in my home.

Oh yes, men are thought of as not showing emotion or worse. They often lash out in rage against anything that could trigger a public display of sorrow. In truth it's not quite that simple. Men of my age were raised with the concept that men are stronger. I read a book in college, *The Natural Superiority of Women*, by Ashley Montagu. It changed my understanding of alleged male supremacy, so I had an advantage in breaking from the norm. I was able to admit my vulnerability as I lay there that day in a puddle of tears. When I began going to a grief support group I noticed how few men were in attendance compared to women. What women may not know is how a man can be just a hair's breadth away from losing that control.

The emotion I find hardest to express is joy. I struggle to allow myself that feeling, for it was so far from sight in those first two years. Even now, six years later, I have a hard time trusting in it. When you have been off the ice for so long, you fear that the ice may be so thin that it will break under your feet. For me it is a struggle to allow myself to go there.

*

DAVID JONES
David's 54-year-old wife Judy
was killed by a drunk driver in 2008

If the relationship is a good one, the longer you are with someone the stronger and better the bond becomes. I could not imagine a better companion than Judy; just thinking of her would always make me feel so incredibly good. Knowing that there is someone who understands you inside and out and still loves you, and would do anything for you is incredibly powerful. At the same time, if you should lose that person it is totally devastating.

In searching for someone to spend the next stage of my life with, I looked for a widow who had a great marriage too, and who was around my own age. I was extremely lucky and found Diane. She is not like Judy, and I am not like her late husband Jeff, but we can embrace while discussing our first spouses with each other, support each other on those hard days, and provide joy, love, and support to each other every day. Don't give up on life; always make the best of the situation you are in.

*

JOHN PETE
John's 71-year-old grandmother Tita died
from diabetes and a series of strokes in 1989

Men and women may express grief differently, and there is nothing wrong with that. It's important for each one to let the other grieve in his or her own way while offering nonjudgmental support according to those individual needs. No one, male or female, should be pressured to grieve in ways that cause more stress. Offering support is very much about being a supportive presence, not about trying to steer someone's grief.

*

ROBERT RIECK
Robert's 18-year-old daughter
Ashley died by suicide in 2016

I would want women to know that I, as a man, try to be strong for all, but we feel emotion so deeply that it engulfs us, but we try to hide it in order to be the rock that everyone thinks we should be. The emotion I have the hardest time expressing is crying in front of people, because men are not supposed to.

*

CHAPTER FIFTEEN

THE FEARS

The oldest and strongest emotion of mankind is fear, and the oldest and strongest kind of fear is fear of the unknown. -H. P. LOVECRAFT

Fear can cut like a knife and immobilize us like a straitjacket. It whispers to us that our lives will never be the same, our misfortunes will manifest themselves again, and that we are helpless. How do we control our fear so it doesn't control us?

*

CHUCK ANDREAS
Chuck's 60-year-old wife Gloria
died unexpectedly from heart disease in 2014

As I have expressed before, my biggest fear growing up was living my life alone, and here I am, doing just that. My best friend (Glor), my parents, and my best male friend are all gone. Don't get me wrong, I have friends and acquaintances, but the people I was closest to are not here anymore. It would be nice to have someone to discuss things with, but all my friends have partners, so it's easier to leave them alone because they have their own problems to deal with. At my age, how do you meet someone? It took me forty years to find someone, and now I'm supposed to start over. It seems like a daunting task. I dislike the word "daunting," but it is, having to go through all those rituals all over again, the expectations, the comparisons. Like I said, it just might be easier to stay alone, because I would not and will not be with someone just because there's no one else; I will not just settle for someone. I don't know if I could open myself up to someone and love her with the possibility of going through this pain all over again.

*

JEFF BALDWIN
Jeff's 20-year-old son Matthew died
in a drowning accident in 2011

I have a problem looking at aboveground pools ever since my son drowned in one. In the beginning I was enraged and contemplated going down and taking a knife to the pool he died in. However, it was always just a contemplation thank goodness. I think of Matt every time I go to the community pool that he swam in the week before he died. He was getting in shape and he was so happy to lose those ten pounds in seven days while he was up here with me for that week.

*

ROBERT BOOS
Robert's 21-year-old son Kevin
was killed by a drunk driver in 2015

Nine p.m. at night and my cellphone rings. I see it's my son or my daughter calling. I'm instantly startled and worried. What's wrong? What happened?

"Dad, I can't figure out how to get this network connection to work," my daughter says.

"Hey, Dad, just saying hello. I'm on my way home from a job,"

188

my son says. Instantly, I swallow my fear and realize it's good to hear from them. I have never had this reaction before. I was never fearful of a phone call.

Of course, that was prior to September 6, 2015.

Now just my phone ringing sets off a fear in my heart. I would normally ignore unknown numbers or numbers that were not saved in my phone. Now I just *have* to answer that phone. Something could be wrong. They are all sales calls, political calls, or some other mindless garbage. Except for one sales call a couple of months after Kevin's death that stung me particularly hard.

"Hello, Mr. Boos. This is Florida State University Alumni Association. Everything is all right with your student, I'm just calling to......"

Ugh. This is just a poor student volunteer who has no idea. He just has a list of former FSU students and he is trying to sell them something as an alumnus. The emotional part of me wants to stop him and tell him that everything is *not* all right with my son, that he was murdered by a drunk driver right down the road from where you are probably sitting on campus on the phone. In fact, you might drive right past there. In fact, your life is probably in danger when you drive home.

But I resist.

No, I tell him, all is not right. Kevin was killed in September by a drunk driver up there. Please take me off your list.

They haven't called again.

Now if I miss a phone call from a family member, I obsess about it until I can call him or her back. What if something happened? So when I'm tied up I will usually text the person, "I can't talk – are you all right?" Of course they are; please call them when you are free. I will never be free of this concern. I worry about everyone in my life, including the over two hundred people who work for me. I'm worried that they are traveling safely and that they are careful. It's an amazing burden to carry.

*

RODNEY CLOUTIER
Rodney's 21-year-old fiancéee Cattie was killed by a drunk driver in 2013, and his premature daughter Dottie died in 2016

For the longest time, I was afraid of losing another child or another fiancée. It is a fear I am working through, and I don't know when or whether I'll ever get over it.

*

M.G. COY
Myrton's 56-year-old wife Maureen
died of heart failure in 2012

I'm afraid of bringing too much of my past to my future happiness. This is a new experience, and I do not want to hurt anyone. Oneness or loneliness is very hard to handle. I am sure there is someone out in this wide world whom I could make happy and she could make me happy. I just have to get out and look around to see.

*

BILL DOWNS
Bill's 21-year-old son Brad and 19-year-old daughter-in-law Samantha were killed by a drunk driver in 2007

I think my greatest fear was that I would lose my whole family. I felt that if I could not protect my three kids, what made me think I could protect the rest of my family? In the eight and a half years since the kids' deaths, I have learned that I cannot make it each day without the faith and belief that my God is in control. As long as I keep my faith strong, my belief in God, there is nothing I cannot face.

*

JAMES FENNELL
James' 21-year-old daughter Lauren
was killed by a drunk driver in 2008

Oddly enough, the loss of my daughter has taught me to dismiss any fears in my life. In the beginning I found it extremely difficult to let my younger daughter out of my sight. To have her enter her car and drive anywhere nearly set me off in a state of panic. I began to tell myself that Amanda deserved the freedom to live her life and make her decisions. I owed this to her, much in the same manner as I owed the same to Lauren. I slowly realized that I needed to trust in God and that would ultimately serve my greatest good.

Six months later, Amanda would leave for college, three states away, and I would see her off with no anxiety and with total trust.

*

JEFF GARDNER
Jeff's 18-year-old daughter Cassidy
was killed by a drugged driver in 2013

My biggest fear is thinking of the possibilities of losing another child. Before I lost Cassidy, I had friends and family who had lost kids, but it was never a daily thought. After losing Cassidy, it is a reality that it could happen any time to anyone.

*

MICHAEL GERSHE
Mike was 8 weeks old when his 28-year-old mom
Barbara was killed by a drunk driver in 1970
Mike was 33 when his 33-year-old best friend John
was killed in a drunk driving crash in 2004

I'm afraid of driving during the holidays, because there are so many drunk drivers out there. I'm fearful of never letting anyone behind the emotional wall I've built over the years and therefore being alone. I know I shouldn't protect myself like this, but seeing my father at my mother's grave is something I can never forget. I'm just really afraid of letting someone see the pain inside my soul. I know I'm missing out on something incredible with someone, and I'm working on overcoming that fear, but as I am beginning to learn, it takes time.

*

CARL HARMS
Carl's mother Myrtle died from malpractice in 2005
Carl's 56-year-old father James was killed by a drunk driver in 2007

Since my father's death, I have become very fearful of driving at night. I have a constant fear of oncoming traffic. I can't escape the fear, and it keeps me home, away from things that I could enjoy. As time has passed, it has become somewhat easier, but that fear is still deep inside, and at times it keeps me from enjoying certain events.

*

STEPHEN HOCHHAUS
Stephen's 51-year-old wife Kathy
died from adult soft tissue sarcoma in 2011

Making the wrong decision has been my biggest fear. Mistakes I made when my wife was alive had fewer consequences than they do now. We were a team and made important decisions together.

My wife could see the results of any decision farther than I could. Her insight kept us safe and financially stable. Perhaps because she was an accountant by trade and a commercial realtor in Canada, I felt safe working the business, since she had made it profitable. Upon her death I was forced into the office which was her domain. I had so much to learn and not a whole lot of money to waste. I had medical bills to recover from, and my computer skills were weak. I didn't have her there any longer to help me make those decisions.

Another fear I had was that of my sons and their children dying. My wife was only fifty-one when she died so suddenly of a very aggressive cancer. She was in perfect health, so I understood how vulnerable we all are. Now that I have been making decisions on my own for six years, my fears about that have lessened, but my fear for my family's safety somehow lingers on.

*

DAVID JONES
David's 54-year-old wife Judy
was killed by a drunk driver in 2008

For me, losing my wife was the worst thing that I could imagine. Now I find myself not afraid of anything, since the worst that could happen already has. In general, I find myself having a little more patience and tolerance. You realize what is important and what is not. I do a lot more volunteering, but I try to balance it with not overdoing it so I still have time for my present wife, children, and grandchildren.

*

JOHN PETE
John's 71-year-old grandmother Tita died
from diabetes and a series of strokes in 1989

Different losses can result in different (and sometimes the

193

same) fears. There is a fear of facing the rest of one's life without a loved one, fear of never seeing him or her again, fear that the painful grief will never end, fear of social situations, fear based in spiritual challenges, and more.

My personal experience is that fears related to losses are alleviated very gradually over time. Although they sometimes make brief reappearances down the road, they generally subside again and become less and less frequent.

*

ROBERT RIECK
Robert's 18-year-old daughter
Ashley died by suicide in 2016

I am afraid of my giving up so I can be with my daughter, as I have lost a part of me, a *big* part of me. I am most afraid of forgetting the memories I have, and had, of my daughter. Most people have already moved on with their normal lives, but mine is not nearly as normal.

*

CHAPTER SIXTEEN

THE QUIET

Heavy hearts, like heavy clouds in the sky, are
best relieved by the letting go of a little water.
-ANTOINE RIVAROL

The endless void left in our loved one's absence remains day and night. When our minds are free from distractions, there is a moment when sorrow fills the void, threatening to overtake us, unleashing the torrent of tears. For some, that moment happens during the day, and for others it comes at night. What time is hardest for you?

*

CHUCK ANDREAS
Chuck's 60-year-old wife Gloria
died unexpectedly from heart disease in 2014

I am not sure if there really is a major difference between morning and night for emotions to rise up. Sometimes the sunrise of a beautiful morning can set things off, because I think of Glor missing the chance to see it. There are times in the afternoon that I hear certain songs or think of memories, and then at night when I'm alone trying to fall asleep, and memories pop up. I really don't have a specific time of day when emotions can percolate; it happens anytime for me. Unfortunately, nothing can really stop a meltdown;

it just has to run its course. I thought that by now the pain would have lessened, but it hasn't. I still have my moments of feeling like I'm back in that fog.

*

JEFF BALDWIN
Jeff's 20-year-old son Matthew died
in a drowning accident in 2011

Morning is the hardest time for me because I remember waking up early and seeing that I had five messages on my machine. I won't sleep in a room with a telephone anymore, because my daughter is the same age as Matt was when I lost him, and I fear that I will get a call that something has happened to her, which I just couldn't take. I will always live with that fear for the rest of my life. It was on a Friday when I got the message that Matt had drowned, and now every week without fail, Friday rolls around and I think about it. Not occasionally, but every week.

*

ROBERT BOOS
Robert's 21-year-old son Kevin
was killed by a drunk driver in 2015

A bereaved mind that isn't a busy mind is a painful mind. The more you can keep occupied with something, the less you will dwell and relive the loss of your child over and over and over.

For me, the hardest time of day is the evening. I can be so busy during the day with work concerns that I don't have a minute to linger on my loss of Kevin. But later in the evening while sitting in bed, mindlessly flipping channels on TV, is the hardest time. It's when my mind starts to wander and I think about it. Depending on the night, or due to some randomness, I focus on different areas.

Some nights I relive the car crash in my mind. You will notice here that I never use the word "accident," because what happened that night was not an accident. It was the deliberate and selfish acts of drunk drivers who caused the deaths of the three young adults we loved so much. I start reliving the accident, even though I was not there. In fact, I did not go to the scene of the accident until four or five months later, just before the drivers were charged. But somehow I kept thinking about it.

My son was in the front seat of the PT Cruiser that night, headed to a Publix supermarket after a busy fantasy football draft. I had sent him a text about the Miami Dolphins and a news story that I knew he would be interested in and that I believe he was reading. The accused driver of the second vehicle was flying down Pensacola Drive in Tallahassee with a blood alcohol level more than three times the limit. He was driving over 100 miles per hour on a city street with a 40 mph posted speed limit. I keep wondering and reliving in my head this movie of the accident—again, one that I did not see. Our kids' car turned left at the light and the Challenger, moving like a bullet, hit them broadside (T-bone) on my son's side.

The coroner said Kevin was immediately unconscious and died quickly. That's supposed to be comforting. I know he had his seat belt on, he was adamant about that. But did he feel anything? Did he know he was going to die? Did he cry out for his mom or dad? Kevin didn't even get pulled out of the car immediately. He was stuck in there for hours, long declared dead and covered with a blanket. Did anyone see him? What about his "friend" who was driving drunk as well, did Kevin say anything to him? The people who filled out witness statements described running up to the car and seeing everyone unconscious. Perhaps they didn't suffer; perhaps it was over in a flash, but it is something I play over and over in my head every day.

*

RODNEY CLOUTIER
Rodney's 21-year-old fiancéee Cattie was killed by a drunk
driver in 2013, and his premature daughter Dottie died in 2016

My birthday is the hardest time. I met my fiancée on my birthday, and my child was to be born around the same time. Not much celebration goes on for it any more.

*

M.G. COY
Myrton's 56-year-old wife Maureen
died of heart failure in 2012

The hardest? Meal time! Eating alone. And I *hate* food shopping. And every time I enter our home, no one is there. I view TV news at mealtime, for the company I guess.

*

BILL DOWNS
Bill's 21-year-old son Brad and 19-year-old daughter-in-law
Samantha were killed by a drunk driver in 2007

The hardest part of my day is driving by the three crosses on the side of the road. Those crosses remind me that the death of my three kids was not simply a bad dream, but in fact it is the reality. It's been almost nine years since the kids' death. Now when I drive by the crosses on the side of the road, I blow the horn three times. It is my way of telling them I will always be their voice.

*

JAMES FENNELL
James' 21-year-old daughter Lauren
was killed by a drunk driver in 2008

At first the quiet time was extremely painful. That is when the realization that my lovely daughter was not here with me anymore became a reality. The painful thoughts were easier to dismiss during busier periods of the day, but the nights were mine and mine alone. My wife at the time was not willing to discuss our mutual loss or share any feelings. She retreated to her mother and siblings. I had no other living family member other than my younger daughter, who was away at school. It was during these days when I discovered that as comforting as other caring people may be, grief is a solitary journey.

My quiet time began to include more and more reading. I discovered many wonderful authors who guided me to meditation as well as manifestation practices, which ultimately led me from the depths of depression to the wonderful life I have at this time.

To this date, over nine years later, I will often awaken at the same time of night when I received the call from the hospital. In the beginning, I would experience the same fear and panic I felt in my heart the night of the accident, and would be awake for the balance of the night. Now when I awaken and see that 3:45 on the digital clock, I just smile and send loving thoughts to my daughter.

The quiet time has become my friend rather than my foe. When I now encounter times of stillness, I utilize the time to send my departed family loving thoughts and open myself up to feel their love in return. We are all here for but a limited time, but the love that we brought onto this planet remains with us forever.

*

JEFF GARDNER
Jeff's 18-year-old daughter Cassidy
was killed by a drugged driver in 2013

Evenings are the hardest time of day for me. I'm usually busy during the morning and afternoon working. In the evening I am usually sharing time with my kids and thinking Cassidy should be here enjoying it with us.

*

MICHAEL GERSHE
Mike was 8 weeks old when his 28-year-old mom
Barbara was killed by a drunk driver in 1970
Mike was 33 when his 33-year-old best friend John
was killed in a drunk driving crash in 2004

I don't really have a time of day when it is the hardest in regard to my mother. To be honest, sometimes the whole day is hard, which is triggered by something that I may see on the news or read an article about a drunk driving fatality. Since Big John and I worked at the same place, sometimes mornings are hard when I drive to campus. I avoid the street he used to live on as much as possible, though.

When I'm home, comfort activities usually include reading, cooking, watching television or maybe playing a video game. Anything that can keep my mind active and distracted works well for me.

*

CARL HARMS
Carl's mother Myrtle died from malpractice in 2005
Carl's 56-year-old father James was killed by a drunk driver in 2007

Early morning hours have become very difficult, knowing that while I sleep the lives of someone I love, family or friends could be slipping away, or, as in the case of my father, they could be tragically ripped from me. When I wake, as the time begins to tick away I become comfortable with the feeling that all is well for now, and then the time approaches again when I will need to close my eyes and sleep. Although it still creeps up on me at times, I try to keep the feeling that those I love and care for know how I feel.

*

STEPHEN HOCHHAUS
Stephen's 51-year-old wife Kathy
died from adult soft tissue sarcoma in 2011

Evenings at home alone would find me free of the distraction of work that had kept me busy enough to hold it together. When you live alone and things slow down, the demons come. They would find me late at night, brought on by triggers that were all around me. Kathy was everywhere I turned. There was not one part of that house which didn't remind me of her being there and how she no longer was. In total exhaustion I would escape to sleep, only to wake and find things unchanged. I would head to work distracted once more by the day's activities. From the beginning of my grief, I began to keep fresh flowers in our home. I think I did it for her, but it also gave me some comfort. Perhaps I found comfort by doing something I know would have pleased her. It became a ritual which continues today, and when I put the flowers in a vase I look at them and see how connected to her I still am. That for me is not a bad thing, for it is still our house and perhaps she appreciates them being there.

I should say that the demons come visiting less and less now, although I doubt they will ever be completely gone.

*

DAVID JONES
David's 54-year-old wife Judy
was killed by a drunk driver in 2008

For the first year, going to bed at night was the hardest. I would wake up around 3 or 4 a.m. and not be able to get back to sleep. Now I try to stay busy. Every morning I get up a little after 6 a.m. and either work out at the gym or else attend a club meeting. I have Rotary Club on Wednesdays and Toastmasters on Thursdays.

During the week I then go to work. On Saturday mornings I meet friends for breakfast, and on Sundays I go to church. I spend the weekend afternoons and evenings with my present wife, Diane, and we try to do fun things. It could be as simple as kayaking, riding our bikes, or taking a walk, or doing something like attending a concert or festival. Of course, seeing our children and grandchildren as often as we can is top priority.

*

JOHN PETE
John's 71-year-old grandmother Tita died
from diabetes and a series of strokes in 1989

There is a drowsy state of waking from sleep that is still sometimes difficult for me, because that's when I often think of lost loved ones. And when you are half asleep there is always a split second of remembering that your loved one is gone all over again, and your heart skips a beat and you feel the full emptiness of their absence. In earlier days, waking up and remembering losses often set a difficult tone for the entire day. But somewhere along the way I learned to refocus and start the day off on a more positive note.

*

ROBERT RIECK
Robert's 18-year-old daughter
Ashley died by suicide in 2016

The hardest times are late at night and first thing in the morning. I wake up and have to be honest and know she is not ever going to be here again in my life. The nights are the worst as we spent so much time together. Now I am not able to tell her I love her, and I wish she would let me give her a hug, but someone who has depression doesn't want one. I wish I could have just given her many hugs and she would have felt my love, and I should never have let her say no. I just didn't want her to feel uncomfortable.

CHAPTER SEVENTEEN

THE SILVER LINING

Even a small star shines in darkness.
-FINNISH PROVERB

In the earliest days following loss, the thought that anything good can come from our experience is beyond comprehension. Yet some say there are blessings in everything. Have you discovered a silver lining in your loss?

*

CHUCK ANDREAS
Chuck's 60-year-old wife Gloria
died unexpectedly from heart disease in 2014

I've only been on this journey for just over six hundred days. I haven't been able to recognize any discoveries so far, so I guess if there are any I will keep looking.

*

JEFF BALDWIN
Jeff's 20-year-old son Matthew died
in a drowning accident in 2011

It has been five years since losing my son. Life goes on with or without him. In moving forward slowly I have managed to turn my son's loss into positive things. In 2013, I created a grief support group on Facebook called Mending Hearts. We have over three hundred and fifty members and we help each other. Some are just starting out on the journey.

A friend of mine, Mickey, once told me to look for the sparks of light that shine from the other angel parents walking ahead, and follow those sparks of light, because they will lead to the other side of this darkness. I have found this to be true. While I have five years of this grief experience, I can relate to every feeling, every question that others just starting out may have. I would tell people who are experiencing grief to surround themselves with people who can relate to them firsthand on the loss. Those will be the most beneficial people to aid you on your journey.

*

ROBERT BOOS
Robert's 21-year-old son Kevin
was killed by a drunk driver in 2015

I would like to offer comfort here to other grieving men who might read this for help, or to any family member trying to help a grieving man deal with this horrible loss.

But a silver lining? A positive spin on the death of my son? Not in the least. Not even I, who used to be able to put a positive spin on anything, can find a silver lining.

It has clarified some things for me, though. It has shown me who my true friends are and who are not true friends but just peripheral friends.

It's brought me closer to my surviving children.

It's brought some wonderful people into my life that I did not know: Morgan's family; the mom, dad and sister of the young lady who was lost along with my son and Vincenzo. It's intensified the friendship I feel with Vincenzo's family.

It's brought some wonderful people in my life through The Compassionate Friends group, both online and in person.

But a silver lining over all? No. Not at all.

*

RODNEY CLOUTIER
Rodney's 21-year-old fiancéee Cattie was killed by a drunk
driver in 2013, and his premature daughter Dottie died in 2016

The silver lining? That's a hard question to answer. The only silver lining that I can possibly think of was that after the death of my daughter I finally ended up getting a job. Other than that, there really isn't one.

*

M.G. COY
Myrton's 56-year-old wife Maureen
died of heart failure in 2012

None. There is no silver lining in the loss of a spouse. My life as a widower has changed drastically. I am not single, I am widowed. My life changed very much. It is a life I am not used to, and not prepared for. It seems to be sliding downhill from what my life was before. I have tried to cope, but help for men is not available. Of twenty-eight books on the subject, only six are for men, and most of those are written by women.

*

BILL DOWNS
Bill's 21-year-old son Brad and 19-year-old daughter-in-law
Samantha were killed by a drunk driver in 2007

The only thing I can say that I would consider a silver lining is this. It has been hell living without my three kids. I would much rather have had my kids, but God took a horrific heartbreaking tragedy and turned it into a positive life-changing event. Not only did this tragedy bring me to Christ; it brought my life to a new mission. It took me four years to realize there was a silver lining. To be not only the voice for my kids, but to be a voice for all victims and those who have lost loved ones for whatever reason. God's mission for me is to restore hope, restore the desire to be a voice not only for those who are hurting but for Him. *I can do all things through Christ that strengthen me* (Philippians 4:13).

*

JAMES FENNELL
James' 21-year-old daughter Lauren
was killed by a drunk driver in 2008

I have learned that people who experienced a "great awakening" in their lives have usually found this renewal through a personal tragedy. Would it not be another tragedy if my Lauren had lived her short and beautiful life and had not left me something in my heart? Never having written poetry before in my life, I wrote this poem to my beautiful daughter the day following her funeral. I believe it best describes my feelings:

On the warmest of days
When for the briefest of moments
You feel a cool breeze touch your cheek
It will be she
Reaching out to provide you comfort

On the darkest of days
When you see a ray of sunshine break through
Providing hope and belief
It will be she
Sending down her love for you

On the coldest of days
When in a terse moment
You feel the warmth of the distant Winter Sun
It will be she reaching down to provide relief

On the most dreary of days
When your thoughts lead you to a comforting remembrance
It will be she
Being there for you

On the stillest of summer nights
When a special star finds its way to your eye
Think of her
For it will be she
Watching over you

For she is not gone
She is here with us still
In all the ways that will touch your life
.........and reach into your soul.

*

MICHAEL GERSHE
Mike was 8 weeks old when his 28-year-old mom
Barbara was killed by a drunk driver in 1970
Mike was 33 when his 33-year-old best friend John
was killed in a drunk driving crash in 2004

The biggest silver lining is that I miraculously survived the car crash that killed my mother. I am blessed to have the opportunity to present my program, The Magic of Life, to prevent others from being impacted by drunk driving. Years ago when I was presenting my program at a middle school in Chicago, a student asked me whether if I could go back in time, I would change anything. A great question from a sixth grader, and it's also a question I struggle with from time to time. On the one hand, I wish my mother were alive and I could know her voice, feel her touch, and hear "I love you, son." But if I am going to find a positive in my grief journey it is that I have the ability to share my story, that I turned a tragedy into something positive, and I don't take that responsibility lightly. On the days I struggle with my own existence, I think of all the good I've been able to do by sharing my story and keeping my mother's legacy alive.

The other silver lining is having Dolly in my life, as she, along with my father, raised me as her own son. Here was a woman who gave up her dreams and raised my brother and me to be the men we are today. She taught me what the human spirit is capable of when it comes to unconditional love no matter what. I shudder to think what my life would be without her, and I am so grateful that somehow she found her way to us.

Regarding Big John's death, I struggled more to find a silver lining. His death impacted so many people and left such a huge hole in our lives. If I had to pick one silver lining, then it would also be being able to share his story during my program. I don't want other people becoming a Big John to their family and friends. Whether it's talking to DUI offenders or high school students, I want them to know his spirit while he lived, but also how he died. If his death can change someone's life and inspire them to stop driving drunk, then yes, I guess that is a silver lining. To be able to represent his family, his friends and share his legacy to prevent others from going through this pain, then my journey, with all its ups and downs, is worth it.

*

STEPHEN HOCHHAUS
Stephen's 51-year-old wife Kathy
died from adult soft tissue sarcoma in 2011

It took more than three years to find a silver lining in anything. For so long I had little optimism in anything about my life. I looked at my future as just surviving day-to-day, and it felt good just to be able to accomplish that. Something began to change in me, however. Slowly I began to notice that not only had I found a way to get through each day, but I was also accomplishing things only my wife could have done. I realized that I was learning how to cook and bake. I had missed her cooking special things for me that I knew I was never going to taste again if I didn't find the way to do it myself. I began to dig through her massive recipe file, and just followed the directions. I knew I had become motivated, and I knew I was taking a larger step forward.

The same feeling happened with bookkeeping, grocery shopping, and other things. I was learning how to do the things she did, and when I looked back at what I was doing I felt good about myself. I still have a lot to learn, but I've had a taste of something that makes me want more. That is indeed a silver lining. I was no longer just surviving. I was making things happen. I even began planning trips for myself as she would have always done. I could actually get off my tail and go places. When I took a trip to Maui last year for my anniversary, that was when I knew I was on my way to living again. I may have had some sad moments in Hawaii, but I also could go to her favorite place on earth and celebrate the day she chose to spend the rest of her life with me. It has been more than five years now that I have been traveling this grief journey. I look back to where I came from and feel pretty good about what I have accomplished. I can only imagine what I'll do tomorrow.

*

DAVID JONES
David's 54-year-old wife Judy
was killed by a drunk driver in 2008

No one knows how the future might have turned out had a traumatic event not occurred. I am very proud of how all my children have coped and have become wonderful adults with their own fulfilling lives. Getting married to Diane expanded my family to include many more wonderful people whom I otherwise would not have met, but I have no way of knowing what other turns my life might have taken if Judy had not died.

Judy was the center of our family, and her death had a profound impact on all of us. She shaped our lives in so many ways, from tea parties with the kids when they were younger to preparing them for college, she nurtured and guided them into becoming wonderful, self-sufficient adults.

Memories are great, but they are no substitute for getting a hug from someone you love unconditionally.

*

JOHN PETE
John's 71-year-old grandmother Tita died
from diabetes and a series of strokes in 1989

I think that losing loved ones is perhaps the worst thing that could happen to many people in life, but it's also unavoidable.

Through my own losses I have grown, changed, and become more compassionate to myself and to the pain of others. The personal growth one can experience in response to painful losses is something I don't know that I would have experienced otherwise.

Losses have incredible power to change a person, often for the better, but sometimes for the worse, too. They present serious choices and crossroads in life.

*

ROBERT RIECK
Robert's 18-year-old daughter
Ashley died by suicide in 2016

I am not sure a silver lining would be a description after losing a daughter to suicide. If I were to describe a silver lining in this it would be that I have learned to be more compassionate to others' feelings. You can say you understand someone's loss, but you never can until you yourself have experienced the loss of a child.

*

It doesn't matter who you love
or how you love, but that you love.

ROD MCKUEN

*

CHAPTER EIGHTEEN

OUR HOPE

Be like the birds, sing after every storm.
-BETH MENDE CONNY

Hope is the fuel that propels us forward, and urges us to get out of bed each morning. It is the promise that tomorrow will be better than today. Each breath we take and each footprint we leave is a measure of hope. So is hope possible in the aftermath of loss? If so, where do we find it?

*

CHUCK ANDREAS
Chuck's 60-year-old wife Gloria
died unexpectedly from heart disease in 2014

Yes, loss has a way of redefining our life, absolutely. The problem right now is that I'm still trying to redefine who I am. I have been Chuck and Glor for so long that I have no idea who just Chuck is. My definition of hope right now is "I hope I find myself," because right now I have no idea who I am.

*

JEFF BALDWIN
Jeff's 20-year-old son Matthew died
in a drowning accident in 2011

To me, hope is never letting go of your grip on life. Hope is found every day when you wake up and you take that next breath, and ask yourself what will today bring? There is always hope; stop and take a look around. Look into people's eyes and you will see we all are struggling to some degree. We all have hope.

*

ROBERT BOOS
Robert's 21-year-old son Kevin
was killed by a drunk driver in 2015

Hope is the thought that there is something better out there. It is the feeling inside you that yearns for something you do not have, and the confidence that it will someday come to fruition. For me, my biggest hope is that I will see Kevin again. Someday when I'm lying on my deathbed and the end is near, I'm going to see a figure come up to my bed with a big smile on his face and feel his warm hand on mine.

"Hi, Dad. I've missed you."

"Kevin? Is that really you?"

"Yes, Dad. I've always been here with you, but now you can see me."

He looks the same as the last time I saw him alive. Happy. Smiling that big grin of his. His hand warm in mine, not that cold hand I held while he lay in his casket.

"Why are you here, Kevin?"

"I'm here to welcome you, Dad. I'm here to tell you to not be afraid."

"I'm not afraid, Kevin. I have looked forward to this day for a long time."

"I know, Dad. It's so good to see you."

That's what I hope for.

*

RODNEY CLOUTIER
Rodney's 21-year-old fiancée Cattie was killed by a drunk
driver in 2013, and his premature daughter Dottie died in 2016

Hope and faith are really the same to me.

*

M.G. COY
Myrton's 56-year-old wife Maureen
died of heart failure in 2012

My hope is to change my lifestyle and seek happiness in my future lifestyle. It has to be different from what I am used to. A big change, but one that is needed. I cannot forget my past, but I need a future to survive.

*

BILL DOWNS
Bill's 21-year-old son Brad and 19-year-old daughter-in-law
Samantha were killed by a drunk driver in 2007

My hope is my faith in God. Knowing God has given me hope, faith and wisdom. I know that by trusting in God, there is nothing I can't do. I seek every day to serve Him, to serve my fellow victims and to be a voice for those whose voices were silenced. That is my hope, to be the very best I can be.

*

JAMES FENNELL
James' 21-year-old daughter Lauren
was killed by a drunk driver in 2008

Hope is trust. I began to trust the course my life had taken, and I also began to realize that I am not the one in the driver's seat. Yes, we all have free will, which is the gift we bring into this lifetime. But we are all subjected to a greater plan, which may or may not be totally understood by all of us on this planet. Many people refer to this as the art of surrender. The term "surrender" does not mean giving up, but rather accepting life as it is. Surrender is the opposite of giving up. It's giving in to who you are; it's not passive, it's active. But I have to trust in the supreme being or the universe for the proper outcome. That's the hitch. And that's the mystery.

A huge awakening was the result of this terrible loss. I awakened to the understanding of eternal love, a love so powerful that it could not be limited to this dimension. As time went by, I began to feel Lauren's love. I now feel her love more than when she was with me here on earth.

*

JEFF GARDNER
Jeff's 18-year-old daughter Cassidy
was killed by a drugged driver in 2013

I hope Cassidy is proud of the actions I take to try to prevent an innocent person from losing his or her life by a selfish act of impaired driving. I hope that I can live my life in a way that makes her proud of me. I mostly hope she knows how much I miss her.

*

MICHAEL GERSHE
Mike was 8 weeks old when his 28-year-old mom
Barbara was killed by a drunk driver in 1970
Mike was 33 when his 33-year-old best friend John
was killed in a drunk driving crash in 2004

I hope I can continue being a son my mother would be proud of, even on the days when I struggle. I hope to find inner peace along this journey, and that if there is a place where we all go after our time here, I will hear from my mom's own voice that she was proud of what I accomplished in life.

I hope I can continue raising awareness about the dangers of drunk driving, not only for my mother and my family but for Big John's family and friends. I hope that people actually listen and it inspires change in their lives. I am hopeful that I can continue sharing the program for as long as possible because I wouldn't want anyone else to go through this grief journey.

*

CARL HARMS
Carl's mother Myrtle died from malpractice in 2005
Carl's 56-year-old father James was killed by a drunk driver in 2007

Through all this tragedy and the new world that I've been forced into, I've come to know hope as my effort to make a difference in at least one person's life. Hope is believing that you can make a difference in a world that continues even when others have stopped. Hope is believing.

*

STEPHEN HOCHHAUS
Stephen's 51-year-old wife Kathy
died from adult soft tissue sarcoma in 2011

Hope is the thought that something better will be in the future.

Hope is an expectation and a dream. How can one have hope without having faith? The two go hand in hand, for faith is to believe in something without the proof that it is so. If I didn't have faith that something would be ahead for me, then hope would lose all meaning. If I had faith that something would happen and it didn't, well, then at least I had hoped and I could pick up the pieces and begin to hope for something else. A dash of optimism drives hope to a higher level. Before my wife died I never gave hope much thought. Her simple philosophy was that if something was meant to happen, then it will happen. I lived that way for many years, so after I was alone and on my own I began to see hope in an entirely new way. I stopped thinking about what *will* happen and began hoping for what *could* happen.

*

DAVID JONES
David's 54-year-old wife Judy
was killed by a drunk driver in 2008

The world is filled with both good and evil. I choose to do what I can to increase the good in the world, help others, and always look for ways to make things better. I try to help and uplift others, and just enjoy being around other people, appreciating the wonderful world we live in, and always looking for beautiful and interesting things. I try to never stop learning, and I have faith that people working together can solve problems and make the world a better place. Everyone has a story to tell, and I love hearing those stories, and sharing a bit of my own when appropriate. Life is hope.

*

JOHN PETE
John's 71-year-old grandmother Tita died
from diabetes and a series of strokes in 1989

Hope means many things to me, and it also changes and evolves. Hope is a foundation for strengthening personal character for me that also offers enlightenment throughout life's journey.

I hope for healing for myself and others. I hope I will see my loved ones again one day, in God's time. I hope for new paths that offer wisdom, strength, courage, peace, and healing. I hope for sustained spiritual faith in the face of adversity. And I hope for new reasons to feel hope through examples set by the lives of others.

Hope for me is largely about more fully experiencing all the things I encounter in my life with purpose and optimism.

*

ROBERT RIECK
Robert's 18-year-old daughter
Ashley died by suicide in 2016

I believe my definition of hope is to keep my depression in check and hope that her death does not drag me under.

*

You don't live in a world all alone.
Your brothers are here too.

ALBERT SCHWEITZER

*

CHAPTER NINETEEN

OUR JOURNEY

Be soft. Do not let the world make you hard. Do not let the pain make you hate. Do not let bitterness steal your sweetness. -KURT VONNEGUT

Every journey through loss is as unique as one's fingerprint, for we experience different beliefs, different desires, different needs, different tolerances, and often we walk different roads. Though we may not see anyone else on the path, we are never truly alone, for more walk behind, beside, and in front of us. In this chapter lie the answers to the final question posed: What would you like the world to know about your journey?

*

CHUCK ANDREAS
Chuck's 60-year-old wife Gloria
died unexpectedly from heart disease in 2014

First off, I would like to thank Kimmy and Alecia for their support in helping me make the decision to do this. I did this hoping that it will someday help someone, because when Glor passed away, I could not find anything to read that really covered the way I felt. I've seen people dying and dead. I've lost my grand-parents and my parents, but nothing prepares you for when you lose your soulmate. Nothing.

I was not used to having a meltdown all of a sudden. It could be driving down the road, walking through the halls at work, or sitting on the couch at home. I even had to leave the grocery store once in the middle of shopping. Your emotions just take over. You can fight it, but your emotions win every time. Now I've come to accept them as moments of remembering how much I truly loved Glor.

They say you become part of a club; that's the way I've heard it described more than once. You really do become more aware of people who have lost their loved ones. It's a look you get from someone, or that extra hug. Please, when you get the opportunity to talk to someone who has unfortunately experienced a loss, please do that. You are not alone, and it really does help to talk to someone who has gone through it. Please don't hold it in like I did.

There was a couple, Frank and Judy, who said, "Just come over to our house. You don't have to say a word, just get out of the house." It helped me open up. I will never be able to thank Alecia and Heather enough for the times they made sure I got out of the house to do something, anything, because the house became my prison. Please don't get me wrong; when I first lost Glor I needed time alone just to try to get myself together. But there comes a time when you need to let go of that security blanket. When you're ready, take a deep breath, open the door, and get outside.

I've been waiting to get over the pain of losing Glor, I don't think I'll ever get over the pain. I'll just learn to live with it. Last but not least, I would like to thank everyone affiliated with this project. It gave me a chance to open up and get things out of me that I've been holding in. Again, thank you for helping me.

*

JEFF BALDWIN
Jeff's 20-year-old son Matthew died
in a drowning accident in 2011

While I will always struggle and cope with my loss in my own way, I would want everyone to know that we all will suffer great loss somewhere in our lifetimes. It may not be as tragic as losing a child, but it's still a great loss. I firmly believe we were spiritual beings before we came to be in this human experience. We learn life lessons from the things that we experience while we are here. These are life lessons that the soul retains, and some day this human experience will come to an end, and we will once again revert to spiritual beings. So as long as we hold on to something that keeps us grounded, we will be okay, whether it be our faith or our beliefs. Never deny yourself your own reason for being here. This is your own spiritual journey, because in the end that is why your soul is here, and once your soul gets what it came for while having this human experience, it leaves.

*

ROBERT BOOS
Robert's 21-year-old son Kevin
was killed by a drunk driver in 2015

I hope that if you are a newly bereaved person or even a "seasoned" bereaved person, you have read some of my stories as well as the stories of the other men in this book and you have gained some insight into this horrible world of grief or you have gained some comfort in some of these words.

I hope that if you have a man in your family or a close male friend and he has suffered a horrible loss, that you can read our words and gain some insight into why he is feeling like he does and how you can best be there for him. I hope that if you haven't lost someone and don't know anyone who has lost someone, you are just reading this book to learn more from us. I hope you remember some of these words someday if grief ever crosses your path.

Grief joined me on the evening of September 6, 2015, and has been a constant companion of mine ever since. At the beginning grief rode on my shoulders and was very heavy. It was also visible for everyone to see. I was clearly carrying this burden.

Weeks after my son's death, grief crawled inside me. It lives mostly in my brain, but makes frequent appearances in my heart and in my lungs. It's always there. It might not be as loud and as brash as it was in the beginning, but it's there for sure.

Anytime I have anything I can celebrate, anytime I am enjoying a trip or a night out, grief makes an appearance. It taps me on the shoulder as if to remind me that it's still there and it isn't appropriate for me to be happy.

"Your son is dead. Have you forgotten?" grief says quietly in my ear.

"No, you're right. I just wasn't thinking about it at the moment." And with that, my enjoyment of the moment is gone and I'm dwelling again on my loss.

I've learned to hide grief quite well. In fact, most people around me at work probably think I'm "over it" and doing much better. Silly people. You are in the midst of an excellent actor, one who should win some kind of award because inside I am completely empty and bare. All of me inside died with my son on that hot September evening in 2015. You are seeing the shell of me with an excellent puppet master inside pulling the strings. You would think I'm a whole person.

I leave you with this: the loss of a child is unfathomable. There are not enough words in the English language to fully explain it to you. If you have not lost a child, you simply don't understand. Losing a parent, a grandparent or a spouse are horrible things. I've lost a parent and all of my grandparents. I miss them all the time. But there was something natural about that. We are expected to bury our grandparents and our parents some day. It's part of being a human being; it's part of life and death. Losing one of your children (at any age) is unnatural. Parents should never have to pick out a casket for their child or decide what outfit they will wear for all of eternity. It just isn't right. My friend Tiffany, who lost her daughter Emma about the same time we lost Kevin, posted about actually throwing some of the dirt on her daughter's casket and how surreal that was. And how now she looks back at it painfully. We didn't do that, so I cannot imagine how difficult that was.

Kevin was a beautiful person inside and out. He was genuinely kind to everyone he met. He went out of his way to make people feel welcome and comforted. He loved sports passionately. He loved his family and his family loved him. He was just hitting his stride as a senior in college. He loved his job and was working out all the time. Then some ex-convict on parole decided to drive drunk and killed my son. Gone instantly, in a flash. No goodbye, no "I love you." Nothing.

That's why grief will be with me for the rest of my life, trying to help me sometimes, but trying to hurt me most other times.

*

RODNEY CLOUTIER
Rodney's 21-year-old fiancéee Cattie was killed by a drunk
driver in 2013, and his premature daughter Dottie died in 2016

Time does heal all wounds and to not drastically change your life over an incident that was out of your control.

*

M.G. COY
Myrton's 56-year-old wife Maureen
died of heart failure in 2012

My journey has been difficult, and my friends and family have realized that. But my journey has been difficult for me, and only I can deal with it, and with my future happiness. And at this point, all I wish for is some kind of happiness in my life.

*

BILL DOWNS
Bill's 21-year-old son Brad and 19-year-old daughter-in-law
Samantha were killed by a drunk driver in 2007

This is not a journey I chose. Someone chose it for me. I would want to tell others that we choose our destiny. It is not predetermined. God will not force His will on you. He lets us make our own choices in life, but when we do, we must be willing to face the consequences of those choices. Life is too short not to live our lives for God. If I believe in God, and I am wrong, I am out nothing. If *you* don't believe in God and *you* are wrong, you have lost your soul. *I choose to believe!*

*

JAMES FENNELL
James' 21-year-old daughter Lauren
was killed by a drunk driver in 2008

Through much meditation, prayer, and reading, I had begun to realize that Lauren had finished her work here on earth. She left behind a cry of torment in my heart. Earlier in my grief I had doubts that I was strong enough to deal with the remains of such inner turmoil. The desolation and horror of this loss seemed to trump any feeling that remained to the contrary. But then I realized that this pain is Lauren's gift to me. No, she would never consciously hurt me in such a manner, but there it was, and it had to work itself through me in order to become the experience and lesson that I needed to learn in this lifetime. Something dies within when a child is lost, and it was only through prayer and meditation that I was able to begin to see it as the supreme being sees it. I began to understand the love of God. I began to bear the unbearable and live my life with the lesson of love that Lauren had left for me. I began to understand that Lauren and I, along with other loved ones, have been helping each other progress our souls for numerous lifetimes.

Then there came a time when my grief found its expression. Most of the time we expect our children to live our legacy. I began to live Lauren's legacy. It was a legacy of love. I began to realize that if we permit ourselves to live according to love, we will be blessed with the all the inner knowing and strength that we need to live our lives in a fulfilling manner. The holding of a door, speaking to an elderly lady in a supermarket who may not have had anyone speak to her all day, placing a dollar in a homeless man's hand—these are all things that pay forward a positive vibration as well as having a ripple effect upon humanity. I try my best to perform positive actions and deeds in Lauren's name.

*

JEFF GARDNER
Jeff's 18-year-old daughter Cassidy
was killed by a drugged driver in 2013

I have been put in groups that I wished I hadn't. I have been put in these groups and organizations and with people who share the same heartache. But since I have, I am so very grateful for AVIDD, 1N3, and MADD, because without their support I am not sure where I would be now. I hope we can continue spreading the word that drunk driving is preventable. And death happens by actions that are senseless and preventable. In Cassidy's school annual, she put a quote on her senior page that said, "In the end it's not the years in your life that matter, but the life that's in your years!" She would lose her life just seven months after graduation!

*

MICHAEL GERSHE
Mike was 8 weeks old when his 28-year-old mom
Barbara was killed by a drunk driver in 1970
Mike was 33 when his 33-year-old best friend John
was killed in a drunk driving crash in 2004

Since my mother was killed when I was an infant, grief has always been a part of my life. I didn't know it at the time, but I grew up with grief. My journey with it is continuous, and I think it will always be prevalent in my life. I don't want people to feel sorry for me, because then I feel like a victim more than a survivor. Sure, I struggle with it, and use humor as a defense mechanism to hide my pain. On the days when I struggle, I want space. On the days when I feel anger, I want more space. And on the good days, I'm probably still hurting, but will never admit it. Actually, I think I just did!

We all manage grief differently, but somehow I did it in a relatively healthy manner. I'm proud that I never turned to alcohol or drugs during my journey. My mother or Big John wouldn't want me to do anything stupid no matter how much I was hurting. The human spirit can take only so much grief before we crack, and that does us no good at all. I'm glad I was blessed with a sense of humor for a healthy way to manage my grief. Always keep your sense of humor, it is a powerful tool in life.

I recently learned, in fact by writing for this book, that I had to ask for help. It wasn't easy, but when I felt like I was buried emotionally and overwhelmed with so much, it was time to swallow my pride and ask for help. I don't want to be a victim of my grief and let it control me. I want to be a survivor of it and control it as much as possible. Asking for help doesn't make you weak, it makes you stronger.

Every day when I wake up, I realize that it's a good day for me. No matter what the weather is like outside or what may come my way at work, I'm alive. I was kept alive for a reason, and I feel like I am living a life of which my mother would be proud. On the days when I struggle the most, I imagine her smiling and bragging to her friends about her son. With each program I do, it helps with my journey, because I believe I'm making a difference in this crazy world.

My grief journey with Big John is slightly different than it is with my mother, because I knew him for fifteen years. From being stupid college kids to young adults, we shared many fun memories together. Along with friends Brent, Bryan, Dennis, and Sean, we were brothers, and we continue to lean on each other to cope with his death if need be. I think one great thing that men do is rely on friends when we need to, especially when we are hurting.

However, what I want the world to know the most is that drunk driving has to stop. I've lost my mother and one of my best friends because of it. I've worked so hard in the last twenty years in presenting The Magic of Life. My journey will continue as long as I am able, because I owe that much to my mother and Big John. Their deaths will not be meaningless. I can help save people from going through their own grief journeys by preventing drunk driving.

*

CARL HARMS
Carl's mother Myrtle died from malpractice in 2005
Carl's 56-year-old father James was killed by a drunk driver in 2007

In this new world, with all the tragedy of having my family foundation ripped from me due to the lack of responsibility of another person, the public perception of responsibility, I've come to see where we are going wrong. The silence caused by this tragedy is constant, and continues because we allow it. Our generation has given up on our future, our children! I will stand and be the voice in our community starting with our future leaders, our youth! For entirely too long we have stood by, allowing these stories of lives lost to just slip by us in the quick headlines of the news. Who will stand and be the voice, who will stand and take action? Lord, here I am! Send me.

We must educate our youth and restore responsibility; we need to fight the stigma and fear that prevent our youth and community from taking responsibility. We have deemed our future irreversible by allowing it to be left unsaid and ignoring where we need to start. There is a lack of responsibility while driving, lack of responsibility with guns, lack of responsibility in respecting each other, lack of responsibility for our babies. There is a no-care attitude and an era of failure. Education and restoring responsibility are the key elements that are missing. With those we will save lives!

It's our W.A.R.; **We Are R**esponsible for our future; we must continue to pray for the strength and knowledge to expand our relationship with our community and understand that God will not do the things we ask of Him if we don't act upon them! I want to provide our community, especially our youth, with the necessary tools to save lives and the strength to speak up when they have knowledge of a crime that has taken place or will take place against another person. It truly takes a village! Responsibility starts in the home and continues through each of us in the community.

"It takes a village" is a proverb that leverages the cultural context and belief that it takes an entire community to raise a child. A child has the best ability to become a healthy adult if the entire community takes an active role in contributing to the rearing of that child. No man, woman, or family is an island. Over the past twenty-five years we have lost our faith in each other, and community isn't always what it is supposed to be. We'd all like to think we live in a place where people care about others, where people pitch in to help when things get rough, where it's safe to leave the doors unlocked and let the kids play outside. But this isn't always what we experience. Instead of community, we find alienation; looking for safety, we are attacked by crime; hoping for a better life for our kids, we encounter alcohol, drugs, gangs, guns, child abuse, domestic violence, human trafficking, rape, and the list goes on and on. People often retreat behind closed double-locked doors and try to ignore their neighbors.

It takes a village, and as a village, it is time we push for progress, working for reconciliation instead of promoting the envy and the hate that divide us further. Let's restore responsibility and be accountable for our future. Responsibility starts with me; responsibility starts with us! The time is NOW. Stand up, do your part! *Then I heard the voice of the Lord saying, "Whom shall I send? And who will go for us?" And I said, "Here am I. Send me!"* (Isaiah 6:8).

*

STEPHEN HOCHHAUS
Stephen's 51-year-old wife Kathy
died from adult soft tissue sarcoma in 2011

I want the world to see what grief is like for me. I want to share a story about the complex living hell I have been going through and yet let you see how I am still standing. I had been married before, and thought I was in love a few times, but when I met Kathy I found what love truly is. I married the most wonderful and beautiful woman on this planet, who showed me how intensely I could be loved. My wife was eleven years younger than me, yet I had found a teacher who brought me higher than I ever thought possible. She challenged me to join her. She was everything I ever wanted to be, and all I had to do was wake up each day and be part of a team like no other. To make love to her was to not know where my body ended and hers began. So connected were we, and what a team we became. When she passed, I was torn in half. So certain was I that I could not survive as half the man I thought I would be, that in those first few years I had no hope at all. Like a badly injured person, I could hardly rise from bed. Life had lost all meaning, and death would be a blessing. So many thoughts go through a man's mind when his world is shattered. So many nights the demons would come, and that was the way I lived. I could walk around my home surrounded by triggers that would destroy me in minutes.

I would also go to work and see her hand on everything that I would touch, yet I was conflicted. How could I feel so badly and hurt so much when I was still alive while that young woman had to die with pain? There I was still here and wishing I could die. With grief counseling and a lot of support I kept going day-to-day until one day I realized that I was still standing and that I smiled more than I cried. I can't remember the day I first noticed that, for I am years down the road now.

Do I still miss Kathy? You bet. There is never a day that goes by when I don't. There isn't a day that goes by when I don't say out loud, "I love you so much, Kath." There is a reason I keep her voice on our answering machine at home. I keep it so I can call from the road and hear her sweet voice once again. I know beyond a doubt that she travels with me. Part of her will always reside inside my very soul, and so with that thought I keep on trying. I owe it to her to make every day count as long as I am still on this earth, and in the words of Queen Noor, "When we meet again at the journey's end, and we laugh together once more, I will have a thousand things to tell you."

*

DAVID JONES
David's 54-year-old wife Judy
was killed by a drunk driver in 2008

I consider myself an ordinary man, who was extremely lucky to find the best of all possible women to become his wife. I had thirty years of the most incredibly fulfilling marriage I can imagine. It is like knowing that you are the richest man in the world, but keeping it a complete secret. Fame and fortune are not nearly as important as love. If you are lucky enough to find it, never let it go and enjoy each minute to the fullest. When you are with the one you love, you each help the other become more than you could be on your own, and by sharing each other's world you make it such a better place.

Secondly, volunteer and help others in any way you can. Donate blood, help at a homeless shelter or food pantry, belong to a church and participate in outreach ministries, help a child to read. Together we can do a lot!

Finally, never give up believing in God and that he is love. This also means believing in yourself, and that you can go on despite all the bad things that have happened. Cherish all the memories you have of those who are no longer with us, and try to build good memories for those you love, knowing that someday they will be remembering you.

This what helped me cope after I lost the love of my life.

Have gratitude for every minute that you had together. Cherish each memory and relive them at appropriate times.

Find purpose for your life. Some of mine are:

God.

Family. I try to help my children and grandchildren. Just be there for them when they need it, but let them live their own lives and blaze their own paths. Celebrate their successes and encourage them after setbacks. See everyone on a regular basis, even when they are in another state, and use phone calls, texts, and email to communicate regularly.

Helping others by sharing my and Judy's story in the most compelling way that I can to prevent DUI drivers from re-offending. I like to think that my actions have saved lives, based on comments after my talks and sometimes feedback from those I meet years later who have successfully changed their lives.

Donate blood. This can help save lives in a very tangible way.

Providing financial support for children in other countries. I sponsor three children in other countries. This allows them to get food and healthcare, attend school, and receive spiritual encouragement.

Working. I feel needed and am able to contribute to my company's success.

Volunteering on a regular basis.

Stay positive. No one can change the past, but you can make choices that will affect the future.

When enough time has passed, remarry if you can find the right person. I missed not being able to do things on a daily basis for someone else. Romance was a huge part of my life, and I really missed it; living in the past was not enough.

Exercising on a regular basis and try to eat healthy.

Having as many friends as possible. For myself this includes:

Staying active in my church.

Joining clubs. I joined Toastmasters and Rotary. I have made a lot of friends in both organizations and attend weekly meetings at both clubs.

Serving on a committee for a food pantry and helping them out as best I can. This is another way of providing tangible benefits to others who need it most.

Meeting others in the neighborhood where I live. My wife and I created a street directory and distributed it afterward. I also worked on a neighborhood float for the Fourth of July parade.

Meeting with a group of friends every Saturday morning for breakfast. Usually there are between four and seven of us who show up to just enjoy friendship and talk.

The best piece of advice I can give that applies to everyone is to communicate frequently with those you care about and to always tell them that you love them every time you talk. The truth is that everyone will die sooner or later, and for the survivors it is so much easier if they have talked recently with the departed and know that they showed their love. Try doing it for a month and see what a difference it makes. After it becomes a habit, often it will spread to others like a big ripple. Such a simple thing, but it can have a profound impact on many lives.

*

JOHN PETE
John's 71-year-old grandmother Tita died
from diabetes and a series of strokes in 1989

My life has been touched and challenged by many personal losses, and I have gradually come to believe that there are great lessons to learn from them. It's very easy to be diminished by losses, but I believe it is so much more important to find ways to learn and grow from them. Loss and grief have taught me that everyone's personal journey is different and unique, and yet perhaps much the same in many ways. To me that says we are all on a unique path, but the bigger purpose is the same.

*

ROBERT RIECK
Robert's 18-year-old daughter
Ashley died by suicide in 2016

The thing about my journey, like that of many of us who have gone through such a tragic time, is not to let the what-ifs, what could have been, and the if only I would haves consume us and our daily lives. It is a hard journey that takes time, and to think that one day you magically wake up and all is good is nonsense. We will never be the same. Our lives have changed drastically, and there is no amount of time to heal the wounds in our hearts and lives. I take one day at a time, and sometimes one minute at a time. I am fine with that, and if others are not, then I ignore their ignorance. It's okay to be sad, it's okay to be emotional, and it's okay to be a man and cry. Just don't let it consume you, because it will if you let it.

CHAPTER TWENTY

FINDING THE SUNRISE

One night in my own journey, I had one of *those* dreams: a vivid nightmare that stays with you. I was running westward in a frantic attempt to catch the sun as it descended below the horizon. Advancing from behind was nightfall; ominous and frightening. It was a pitch-black abyss. And it was coming directly for me. I ran desperately as fast as my legs could go toward the sunset, but my attempt was futile; it sank below the horizon, out of my reach. Oh, the looming nightfall was terrifying! But it was clear that if I wanted to see the sun ever again, I had to stop running west and instead walk east to begin my journey through the great nightfall of grief. For just as there would be no rainbow without the rain, the sun rises only on the other side of night.

The message was clear: it was futile to avoid my grief; I had to allow it to swallow me whole. Then, and only then, would I find my way through it and out the other side.

I remember reading in a bereavement book that if we don't allow ourselves to experience the full scope of the journey, it will come back to bite us. I couldn't fathom how it could get any worse, but I knew I didn't want to test that theory. So I gave in and allowed the grief to swallow me whole. I allowed myself to wail on my daughter's bedroom floor. I penned my deep emotions, regardless of who read them. I created a national radio show to openly and candidly discuss our journeys with anyone who wanted to call in. And I allowed myself to sink to the bottom of the fiery pits of hell. This, in turn, lit a fire under me to find a way out.

Today I'm often asked how I manage my grief so well. Some assume that because I have found peace and joy, I'm simply avoiding my grief. Others believe that because I work in the bereavement field, I'm wallowing in self-pity. Well, which is it?

Neither. I miss my child with every breath I take. Just like you, I will always have my moments and triggers: the painful holidays, birthdays, death anniversaries, a song or smell that evokes an unexpected memory. But I have also found purpose, beauty and joy again. It takes hard work and determination to overcome profound grief, and it also takes the ability to let go and succumb to the journey. Do not be afraid of the tears, sorrow, and heartbreak; they are a natural reaction and imperative to our healing.

As you walk your own path, avail yourself of whatever bereavement tools ease your discomfort, for each one was created by someone who walked in your shoes and understands the heartache. While there are many wonderful resources available, what brings comfort to one person might irritate the next. Bereavement tools are not one-size-fits-all, so if one tool doesn't work, find another.

Lastly, grief is not something we get *over*, like a mountain. Rather, it is something we get *through*, like the rapids of Niagara Falls. Without the kayak and paddle. And plenty of falls. But it's also survivable. And if others have survived this wretched journey, why not me? And why not you?

On the following pages are the baby steps I took to put hell in my rearview mirror. At first they took great effort and lots of patience. But like any dedicated routine, it got easier over time, and the reward of finding balance in my life was worth every step.

1. VALIDATE YOUR EMOTIONS

When we talk about our deep heartbreak, we aren't ruminating in our sorrow or feeling sorry for ourselves. By discussing it, we are actually processing it. If we aren't allowed to process it, then it becomes silent grief. Silent grief is deadly grief.

Find a friend who will patiently listen while you discuss your loss for fifteen minutes every day. Set the timer, and ask him or her not to say anything during those fifteen minutes. Explain that it is important for you to just ramble without interruption, guidance, or judgment. You need not have the same listener each time, but practice this step <u>every</u> day.

2. COMPASSIONATE THOUGHTS

Find yourself a quiet spot. It can be your favorite chair, in your car, in your office, or even in your garden. Then clear your head and for five minutes think nothing but compassionate thoughts about yourself. Not your spouse, not your children, not your coworkers, but yourself. Having trouble? Fill in the blanks below, and then give yourself permission to really validate your positive qualities. Do this every day.

I have a _____
Example: good heart, gentle soul, witty personality

I make a _____
Example: good lasagna, potato salad, scrapbook, quilt

I'm a good_____
Example: friend, gardener, knitter, painter, poem writer

People would say I'm _____
Example: funny, kind, smart, gentle, generous, humble, creative

3. TENDER LOVING CARE

While grieving, it is important to consider yourself as being in the intensive care unit of Grief United Hospital, and treat yourself accordingly. How would ICU nurses treat you if you were their patient? They would be compassionate, gentle, and allow for plenty of rest. That is exactly how you should treat yourself. Also, consider soothing your physical self with tender loving care as an attentive way to honor your emotional pain. This doesn't mean you have to book an expensive massage. If wearing fuzzy blue socks offers a smidgen of comfort, then wear them unabashedly. If whipped cream on your cocoa offers a morsel of pleasure, then indulge unapologetically. Treating our five senses to anything that offers a perception of delight might not erase the emotional heartache, but it will offer a reminder that not all pleasure is lost.

List five ways you can offer yourself tender loving care, and then incorporate <u>at least three</u> into your day, every day. With practice, the awareness of delight eventually becomes effortless, and is an important step toward regaining joy. TLC suggestions:

- Shower or bathe with a lovely scented soap
- Soak in a warm tub with Epsom salts or a splash of bath oil
- Wear a pair of extra soft socks
- Light a fragrant candle
- Listen to relaxing music
- Apply a rich lotion to your skin before bed
- Indulge in a few bites of your favorite treat
- Enjoy a mug of your favorite soothing herbal tea
- Add whipped cream to a steaming mug of cocoa
- _____
- _____
- _____
- _____

4. SEE THE BEAUTY

Listening to the birds outside my bedroom window every morning was something I had loved since childhood. But when Aly died, I found myself deaf and blind to the beauty around me. My world had become colorless and silent. One morning as I struggled to get out of bed, I halfheartedly noticed the birds chirping outside my bedroom window. My heart sank as I realized that they had been chirping all along, but I was now deaf to their morning melody. Panic set in as I concluded that I wouldn't enjoy life's beauty ever again. Briefly entertaining thoughts of suicide to escape the profound pain, I quickly ruled it out. My family had been through so much already; I couldn't dump further pain on them. But in order to survive the heartbreak, I had to find a way to allow beauty back into my life.

So on that particular morning as I lay in bed, I forced myself to listen and really *hear* the birds. From that point forward, every morning I repeated that same exercise. With persistent practice, it became easier, and then eventually effortless, to appreciate the chirping and singsongs.

Profound grief can appear to rob our world of all beauty. Yet the truth is that despite our suffering, beauty continues to surround us. The birds continue to sing, flowers continue to bloom, the surf continues to ebb and flow. Reconnecting to our surroundings helps us to reintegrate back into our environment.

Begin by acknowledging one small pleasantry each day. Perhaps your ears register the sound of singing birds. Or you catch the faint scent of warm cookies as you walk past a bakery. Or notice the sun's illumination of a nearby red rosebush. Give yourself permission to notice one pleasantry, and allow it to *really* register.

Here are some suggestions:

- Listen to the birds sing (hearing)
- Observe pretty cloud formations (sight)
- Visit a nearby park and listen to the children (hearing)
- Notice the pretty colors of blooming flowers (sight)
- Light a fragrant candle (scent)
- See the beauty in the sunset (sight)
- Attend a local recital, concert, play, or comedy act (hearing)
- Wear luxury socks (touch)
- Wrap yourself in a soft scarf or sweater (touch)
- Indulge in whipped cream on your cocoa (taste)
- Enjoy a Hershey's chocolate kiss (taste)

5. PROTECT YOUR HEALTH

After our daughter's accident I soon found myself fighting an assortment of viruses including head colds, stomach flu, sore throats and more, compounding my already frazzled emotions. Studies show that profound grief throws our body into flight-or-fight syndrome for months and months, which is very hard on our physical bodies. Thus, it becomes critical to guard our physical health. Incorporating a few changes into our daily routine feels hard at first, but soon gets easy. Plus, a stronger physical health helps to strengthen our coping skills.

Below are a few suggestions to consider adding to your daily routine to help your physical self withstand the emotional upheaval.

- Practice good sleep hygiene
- Drink plenty of water
- Take a short walk outside every day
- Resist simple carbohydrates
- Keep a light calendar, guard your time carefully
- Don't allow others to dictate and overflow your schedule

6. FIND AN OUTLET

For a long time in the grief journey, everything is painful. In the early days, just getting out of bed and taking a shower can be exhausting. Housecleaning, grocery shopping, and routine errands often take a back seat or disappear altogether. As painful as it is, it's very important to find an outlet that gets you out of bed each day. Finding something to occupy your mind and soothe your senses can be tricky, but possible. Performing a repetitive action can calm your mood, and even result in a new craft or gifts to give.

Beginning a new outlet may feel exhausting at first, but remember that the first step is always the hardest. And you don't have to do it forever, just focus on it for the time being. Possible activities include:

- Volunteer at a local shelter
- Coach a youth's sports team
- Learn a new sport such as golf or kayaking
- Create a memorial garden in a forgotten part of the yard
- Take up woodworking
- Doodle or draw
- Mold clay
- Start a coin or stamp collection
- Join a community civic club such as Rotary

Grief is hell on earth. It truly is. But when walking through hell, your only option is to keep going. Eventually the hell ends, the dark night fades to dawn, and the sun begins its ascent once again.
Just keep going and you, too, will find the sunrise.

Lynda Cheldelin Fell

We can't help everyone,
but everyone can help someone.

RONALD REAGAN

*

THROUGH THE EYES OF MEN

MEET THE WRITERS

*

CHUCK ANDREAS
Chuck's 60-year-old wife Gloria
died unexpectedly from heart disease in 2014

Chuck Andreas was born in upstate New York in August 1953. He spent his early years in Sackets Harbor and Owego, New York, as the oldest of a sister and three brothers. After high school he spent three years in the Army as a military policeman. Upon ending his enlistment he attended Tompkins-Cortland Community College and Binghamton University. He then settled in Endicott, New York, and married for the first time.

Chuck worked for a cleaning company at I.B.M. for the next seventeen years and became president of the local union. After a couple attempts at marriage with children, while divorced Chuck met Gloria Bender on St. Patrick's Day

1995. That was the turning point in his life; he had finally found what he had been looking for. Very rarely did they spend time apart, and they enjoyed their time together. Over the next nineteen-plus years they were apart for only nine days, which breaks down to one day every two years that they were not together until that fateful morning of December 19, 2014.

*

JEFF BALDWIN
Jeff's 20-year-old son Matthew died
in a drowning accident in 2011
JeffEbaldwin@gmail.com
Facebook.com/NewOutlookDrugAlcoholAwareness
Facebook.com/groups/MendingHeartsGriefSupportGroup

Jeff Baldwin was born in Gibsonville, North Carolina, and has spent the past sixteen years in Greensboro. In his spare time he runs a grief support group on Facebook for parents who have lost a child. He also has a Facebook page to spread awareness on the dangers of drugs and alcohol to teens and adolescents. Please like both links above.

Jeff is passionate about spreading the awareness in middle schools and high schools across the country, and believes that education starts at home.

*
ROBERT BOOS
Robert's 21-year-old son Kevin
was killed by a drunk driver in 2015
rvboos@gmail.com

Robert "Bob" Boos has been a leader in hospital finance for over twenty years. He has worked in many leadership roles and is currently the vice president of a two hundred and fifty employee organization in Tucson, Arizona. Bob graduated from the University of Phoenix with a degree in Healthcare Administration. He and his fiancée, Michelle, have five children, aged twenty-six, twenty-five, twenty-four, twenty-three and twenty-two. Kevin, the youngest boy, was killed by a drunk driver on September 6, 2015.

Bob hopes to use his incomparable loss to help other men and women who are grieving the loss of a child. He finds that the only solace in this grief journey is helping other bereaved parents.

Please contact him at rvboos@gmail.com if there is anything he can do for you.

*

RODNEY CLOUTIER
Rodney's 21-year-old fiancée Cattie was killed by a drunk
driver in 2013, and his premature daughter Dottie died in 2016

Rodney Cloutier was born and
raised as what most people call a
military brat. During the first three
years of his life, he had traveled to
places not many people ever see.
After high school he worked to
have a house and family and after
doing so in 2007, he and his wife
were blessed with his first child, a
stepson, and another child the
following year until his divorce in
2009.

Rodney is now a mechanic and
drives a semi. He lives in Buffalo where he and his future wife raise
four kids together, and hope that his first son will come home
someday.

*

M.G. COY
Myrton's 56-year-old wife Maureen
died of heart failure in 2012

M.G. Coy is a retired telephone communication technician. He married Maureen in 1983, and were together for thirty-five years. He now lives alone in a three-bedroom, three-bath, two-car garage in Milford, New Hampshire. He is having a hard time dealing with his loss, and sees a therapist on a weekly basis, trying to deal with it. He became an electronic tech after graduating. He has four children and is still in touch with his two girls, one of whom is in the Army. The youngest has a Master's in criminology.

*

BILL DOWNS
Bill's 21-year-old son Brad, 19-year-old daughter-in-law
Samantha, and 24-year-old family friend Chris
were killed by a drunk/drugged driver in 2007
Advocatesforvicitimsofimpaireddriving.org
avid4duivictims@cableone.net

Bill Downs was born and raised in southern Mississippi, where he met and married his wife, Julie, in 1982. God blessed them with two children, Cynthia and Brad. Bill is twice retired, first from the Air National Guard in 2006 and then from the Gulfport City School District in 2015. His wife is self-employed, and also cares for their handicapped daughter, Cynthia. In 2007, when their son Brad, Brad's wife Samantha, and Chris, a young man they loved as a son, were killed by a drunk driver, their focus turned to advocating and supporting victims of impaired driving. Bill is president and co-founder of Advocates for Victims of Impaired/Distracted Driving (AVIDD), a nonprofit organization. He is also an administrator of four online support groups for victims, and hosts an educational class called AVIDD Voices, where victims share stories with offenders who are court-ordered to attend. Bill is dedicated to the fight against impaired driving, and hopes one day to see an end to this preventable crime that is the only socially acceptable form of homicide.

*

JAMES FENNELL
James' 21-year-old daughter Lauren
was killed by a drunk driver in 2008

James Fennell was born in New York City and raised on Long Island. He earned a BBA from Hofstra University in 1971, and worked in a management capacity for several national retailers before going into his own sales and marketing business in 2004. He is still an active managing partner in his business.

*

JEFF GARDNER
Jeff's 18-year-old daughter Cassidy
was killed by a drugged driver in 2013

Jeff Gardner has lived his entire life in Chattooga County, Georgia.

He graduated from Trion High School in 1991. He has five kids, four of whom are living and one who is in heaven with his mother and sister. Jeff's oldest son is twenty-three-year-old Zach, his daughter Cassidy is forever eighteen in heaven, Emarey is nine years old, Staven is eight, and Gunnar is six. Jeff is married to his soulmate, Tabatha. He works as a brick mason and spends most of his time watching his kids play sports and engage in other hobbies.

*

MICHAEL GERSHE

Mike was 8 weeks old when his 28-year-old mom Barbara was killed by a drunk driver in 1970; Mike was 33 when his 33-year-old best friend John was killed in a drunk driving crash in 2004

www.themagicoflife.org | info@themagicoflife.org

Michael Gershe was born in Suffern, New York, and moved to Miami in 1975, where he lived until he left for college. Despite breaking nearly every bone in his body in a drunk driving crash when he was an infant, he earn a swimming scholarship to Ashland University in Ohio, where he earned a degree in communications. He also attended the University of Akron, earning a Master's degree in Higher Education Administration and began performing standup comedy. While in graduate school he created The Magic of Life program, which combines standup comedy and his story for an inspirational "non-doom and gloom" alcohol awareness and impaired driving prevention program. He has been speaking for over twenty years at schools, colleges, military bases and courts. He is also the senior adviser for the College of Applied Engineering at Kent State University. In April 2015, he founded The Magic of Life, a nonprofit dedicated to preventing impaired driving and helping those impacted by it. Michael is a fan of the Miami Hurricanes, a frustrated fan of the Miami Dolphins, and a member of the KISS Army.

*

CARL HARMS
Carl's mother Myrtle died from malpractice in 2005
Carl's 56-year-old father James was killed by a drunk driver in 2007
www.JAXImpact.org * CHarms@JAXImpact.org

Carl Harms was born and raised in Jacksonville, Florida. After graduating from Edward H. White High School, Carl married, adopted his two beautiful children and bought his home only a few lots down from his parents on the same street he grew up on; life had begun. Carl began a career in municipal parking administration in 1991 while attending Florida State College. In 1993, he earned his firefighter and EMT certifications and spent the next five years as a volunteer lieutenant firefighter and EMT with the Jacksonville Fire and Rescue Department. He left the department following the Florida wildfires of 1998, and continued to build his career in municipal parking administration in Daytona Beach. Realizing that time with his family was limited, Carl resigned from his area manager position and returned to Jacksonville in 2003.

Tragically, he faced the untimely loss of his mother in 2005. He spent the next two years at his father's side until the next tragic chapter, when his father was killed in a four-car collision involving two separate drunk drivers. Carl is now a victim advocate with the State Attorney's Office, 4th Judicial District, and founder/speaker of a community awareness organization, IMPACT! #RestoreResponsibility (JAXImpact).

*

STEPHEN HOCHHAUS
Stephen's 51-year-old wife Kathy
died from adult soft tissue sarcoma in 2011

Stephen Hochhaus was born in December 1948 in Douglas, Arizona, and moved with his family to Phoenix at the age of ten. He developed a love for art, thanks to his aunt who taught and nurtured him. He also developed a passion for flying, thanks in no small part to his father who flew bombers in world war II and owned a family plane. Stephen received his pilot's license at age eighteen and his commercial license by age twenty. Stephen graduated from Arizona State University with a bachelor's degree in art and married his first wife in 1970. The couple had two sons and would later divorce in 1990. Stephen started his picture framing business in 1972, which he still operates today. In 1981 he partnered in an airplane with a gallery owner, transporting artwork around the Southwest. His partner died suddenly in 1991, and Stephen kept the airplane, which he still flies today.

Stephen met his wife Kathy, Canadian by birth, in 1995, when she began doing accounting for his company, and as he would say, "It was magic." They married in 1998 on the anniversary of the day they first met.

*

DAVID ALLAN JONES
David's 54-year-old wife Judy
was killed by a drunk driver in 2008

David Jones grew up in Reynoldsburg, Ohio, and earned a B.A. in Political Science from Ohio State University. He has forty years of experience working in IT.

He is active in church, Rotary, Toastmasters, and with a local food pantry. David speaks against drunk driving to an average of 1,500 people every year for MADD and Maryhaven. He is married and has seven children and eleven grandchildren.

*

JOHN PETE
John's 71-year-old grandmother Tita died
from diabetes and a series of strokes in 1989
griefencounters@aol.com | Facebook.com/peacehopehealing

John Pete grew up in rural Colorado and Texas in a very tightknit extended family. He became a grief counselor in 2004 and has been featured on Open to Hope Radio. His articles "The Gift," "Preparing to Say Goodbye," and "Other Challenges of the Heart" were published in the 2011 book *Open to Hope: Inspirational Stories of Healing After Loss*. He is also quoted throughout "Grieving the Sudden Death of a Loved One" (2012, DVD), and many of his articles are published online.

John was an early advocate of internet grief support and continues to provide outreach and support to others who are struggling with devastating losses and painful grief.

*

ROBERT RIECK
Robert's 18-year-old daughter
Ashley died by suicide in 2016

Robert Rieck is the father of five daughters. He owns several businesses, but considers himself just a typical father who loves his daughters more than anything, and family is the most important thing. Robert did not have a great childhood, to say the least, and has always tried to do the opposite of what was done in his childhood.

THANK YOU

I am deeply indebted to the writers of *Grief Diaries: Through the Eyes of Men*. Such a collaboration sheds crucial insight into the hidden world of male bereavement, offering comfort to other men who find themselves on the same path while helping family and friends to better understand. It required tremendous courage for each writer to bare such vulnerability about a topic so sensitive. I'm humbled to partner with coauthors David Jones and Stephen Hochhaus, two men I admire immensely for their dedication to plowing the field and planting the seeds of hope to benefit others for generations to come.

Finally, there simply are no words to express how blessed I am to be surrounded with love and support from my husband Jamie, our children, and our wonderful family and friends. None of this would have been possible without their wholehearted love that continues to surround me.

Helen Keller once said, "Walking with a friend in the dark is better than walking alone in the light." By sharing our struggles, we learn that we aren't truly alone as we travel our journey, for there are others ahead of us, behind us, and right beside us. That is what Grief Diaries is all about.

Lynda Cheldelin Fell

Shared joy is doubled joy;
shared sorrow is half a sorrow.

SWEDISH PROVERB

*

ABOUT

LYNDA CHELDELIN FELL

Considered a pioneer in the field of inspirational hope in the aftermath of loss, Lynda Cheldelin Fell has a passion for creating and producing groundbreaking projects that create a legacy of help, healing, and hope.

She is an award-winning and international bestselling author of the 5-star book series *Grief Diaries* featuring the poignant true stories by over 500 men and women from 11 countries.

Lynda has interviewed Dr. Martin Luther King's daughter, Trayvon Martin's mother, sisters of the late Nicole Brown Simpson; Pastor Todd Burpo of Heaven is For Real, CNN commentator Dr. Ken Druck, and other societal newsmakers on finding healing and hope in the aftermath of life challenges. She is a national commentator for The Blaze network, CEO of AlyBlue Media, board president of the National Grief & Hope Coalition, and host of the National Grief & Hope Convention 2015.

Lynda's own story began in 2007, when she had an alarming dream about her young teenage daughter, Aly. In the dream, Aly was a backseat passenger in a car that veered off the road and landed in a lake. Aly sank with the car, leaving behind an open book floating face down on the water. Two years later, Lynda's dream became reality when her daughter was killed as a backseat passenger in a car accident while coming home from a swim meet. Overcome with grief, Lynda's forty-six-year-old husband suffered a major stroke that left him with severe disabilities, changing the family dynamics once again.

The following year, Lynda was invited to share her remarkable story about finding hope after loss, and she accepted. That cathartic experience inspired her to create ground-breaking projects spanning national events, radio, film and books to help others who share the same journey feel less alone. Now one of the foremost healing experts in the United States, Lynda is dedicated to helping ordinary people share their own extraordinary stories of survival and hope in the aftermath of loss.

Because of that floating book her daughter left behind, Lynda understands that the dream she had in 2007 was a glimpse into a divine plan destined to bring comfort, healing and hope to people around the world.

lynda@lyndafell.com | www.lyndafell.com | www.griefdiaries.com

ABOUT THE SERIES

It's important that we share our experiences with other people. Your story will heal you, and your story will heal somebody else. -IYANLA VANZANT

Grief Diaries is a ground-breaking series of anthology books featuring true stories about real life experiences. The collection of stories highlights the spirit of human resiliency, explores intimate aspects of each experience, and offers comfort and hope to those who share the same path. The series began with eight books exploring losses shared by people around the world. Over a hundred people in six countries registered, and the books were launched in December 2015. Now home to more than 500 writers in 11 countries, Grief Diaries has twenty titles in print. Another twenty titles are set to be added in 2017.

Now a 5-star series, a portion of profits from every book in the series goes to national organizations serving those in need.

Humanity's legacy of stories and storytelling is the most precious we have. All wisdom is in our stories and songs.

DORIS LESSING

*

ALYBLUE MEDIA TITLES

PUBLISHED
Grief Diaries: Project Cold Case
Grief Diaries: Surviving Loss of a Spouse
Grief Diaries: Surviving Loss of a Child
Grief Diaries: Surviving Loss of a Sibling
Grief Diaries: Surviving Loss of a Parent
Grief Diaries: Surviving Loss of an Infant
Grief Diaries: Surviving Loss of a Loved One
Grief Diaries: Surviving Loss by Suicide
Grief Diaries: Surviving Loss of Health
Grief Diaries: How to Help the Newly Bereaved
Grief Diaries: Through the Eyes of Men
Grief Diaries: Through the Eyes of an Eating Disorder
Grief Diaries: Loss by Homicide
Grief Diaries: Loss of a Pregnancy
Grief Diaries: Living with a Brain Injury
Grief Diaries: Hello from Heaven
Grief Diaries: Grieving for the Living
Grief Diaries: Shattered
Grief Diaries: Poetry & Prose and More
Grief Diaries: Through the Eyes of D.I.D.
Grammy Visits From Heaven
Faith, Grief & Pass the Chocolate Pudding
Color My Soul Whole

FORTHCOMING TITLES (PARTIAL LIST):
Heaven Talks to Children
Grief Reiki
Grief Diaries: Through the Eyes of a Funeral Director
Grief Diaries: You're Newly Bereaved, Now What?
Grief Diaries: Life After Organ Transplant
Grief Diaries: Raising a Disabled Child
Grief Diaries: Living with Rheumatic Disease
Grief Diaries: Through the Eyes of Cancer
Grief Diaries: Loss of a Client
Grief Diaries Life After Rape
Grief Diaries: Living with Mental Illness
Grief Diaries: Living with PTSD

There is a bright future for you at every turn,
even if you miss one.

*

To share your story in a Grief Diaries book,
visit www.griefdiaries.com

PUBLISHED BY ALYBLUE MEDIA
Inside every human is a story worth sharing.
www.AlyBlueMedia.com